1000 GIFTS
FROM A
7x10

Amy Landers-Kearney

press

*"Am I a secret, Amy?
I feel like a secret."*

*"No Dad, you are not a secret.
You never were."*

1,000 GIFTS FROM A 7 X 10

Copyright © 2023 by Amy Landers-Kearney
Waterloo, IA

All rights are reserved. This book is copyrighted. No portion of it may be reproduced, stored in a retrieval system, or transmitted in any form or by any means — electrical, mechanical, electrostatic, magnetic tape, photocopying, recording, or otherwise — without the prior written permission of the author.

ISBN softcover: 979-8-9857473-5-5

DRL Press, Georgetown, Texas

Design and Production: Riverstone Group, LLC

CONTENTS

Introduction 7

Dedication 9

1   Who Was Inmate 05177-046? 11

2   City to City and Oh the Adventures 23

3   The Standoff 45

4   The County Jails 53

5   In Prison on the Outside 59

6   Unknown Caller 75

7   Returning to the War Room 101

8   Compassionate Release — Is There Compassion? 107

9   The Parking Lot 117

10 Compassion 133

11 Dad Came Home 139

12 Faith Remains 155

13 Landers Family Photos, Letters, Mementos 163

14 Supporting Letters 177

15 Final Thoughts 187

INTRODUCTION

Can you list 1,000 things you are thankful for right now in your life? Could you name just 100 things, or even 50?

My quest for this book is to share who Russell Dean Landers was, despite the headlines. I want to share what he meant to me, the depth of despair a daughter feels as she also "does the time" with a father in prison, and to impact change for the incarcerated and the Compassionate Release process in honor of my daddy.

I pray that *1,000 Gifts from a 7X10* will remind you, the reader, that no matter where you lay your head tonight, there is hope.

Throughout these chapters, you will be taken through actual events and stories directly through my life experiences, letters, and phone calls from my dad to demonstrate his passion, his heart, and his love for life, despite living in one of the darkest holes in America—the *Communications Management Unit* in Terre Haute, Indiana.

My journey to publication began when two boxes arrived at my door in mid-April 2020, approximately three weeks after my father passed away. Within his belongings, I found a page folded in half the long way, with numbers going down both columns on the page and titled 1,000 Gifts. My oldest son, Alex commented, "Mom, this is it. This is the title of your book. You have to tell Grandpa's story." This comment spoke to my soul.

I am writing this book to share the story of a man—my father, Russell Dean Landers. He was so much more than inmate #05177-046.

This is his story, from my perspective, from his perspective.

It should be noted, this is my perception, my life with an incarcerated father. My father had unique beliefs, and my authoring of this book does not indicate in any way my belief in the guilt or innocence of my father. This is simply our story.

DEDICATION

To my daddy: May your story impact the hearts of those who have the authority to make sure this never happens again. May you be honored. Thank you for never giving up hope and leaving me a legacy of your relationship with Jesus.

To my mommy: Becky Landers—For your steadfast stability and strength to ensure I grew and found my way. I owe it all to you.

To my children: Alex, Ben, Ava, Jade and my granddaughter, Stella—You are my reasons, the grace you have given me for my faults, your unconditional love and your fight for what's right. Listening and being part of the story. I love you.

To Danny: You came into my life and have been a calmness to my heart when I needed it more than you will ever know. Thank you for taking your place in my life so boldly and with a heart full of love. You are an answered prayer.

To my brothers: Ryan, Mike and family—our story was unique, and powerful. Ryan, my brother in heaven—so many memories of our childhood. Thank you. You stayed focused on your dreams and desires, not letting the life of others distract you—one of the many lessons you taught me. Mike, your laughter, your ability to live life to the fullest and the heart you showed me through this experience was unmatchable. You are truly one of a kind.

To my best friend and Pastor of Hope City Church, and church family, Waterloo, IA: Angela & Pastor Quovadis Marshall — Your support, prayers and walking through life with me has helped mold me into the person I am today. Our friendship is like no other. Hope City, you are family.

To my Ride or Dies: Jessica, Red, Sarah, Chrissy & Lisa — Your friendship means the world to me. I love doing life with you. Your support throughout my life has ensured I made it to the next day.

To Paris Foy: Your love for a man you only knew through me. Thank you for loving my daddy.

CHAPTER 1

Who was Inmate 05177-046?

How do you sum up a life? How do you collect all the fragile pieces? How do you tell the story of someone who meant the world to you and do the story any justice? I don't know, but I am going to do my best.

Russell Dean Landers: a son, father, brother, grandfather, great-grandfather, and faithful son to the King of Kings.

With everything in him he wanted to leave a legacy, so that when he was gone from this earth, his legacy would outlast the years he was given. He wanted so badly to help others discover their purpose, to be exactly who they were called to be. He left me a legacy of his relationship with Jesus, and for this I am eternally grateful, and I assure you as I write, this will not stop with me. How do I ever thank my dad enough for leading so many to the Lord? Myself, my children, and so many that he merely had a conversation with.

Russell was born on November 5, 1949, to the proud parents, Ardean and Inez Landers in Charles City, Iowa. The eldest of three children to this marriage, which includes two sisters, Arlene and Myrna. He was raised on a farm in rural Iowa and spent his childhood helping on the farm, planting corn with his dad and helping with the everyday duties it takes to run a farm. He participated in the Lutheran faith and attended church regularly. In his free time, he learned to play the trombone, and participated in football. He graduated from Greene High School, (Iowa) a small graduating class in 1967.

Russell continued his education earning an associate degree from Ellsworth Community College (Iowa Falls), and a Bachelor of Arts Degree from the University of Northern Iowa (Cedar Falls) in 1973, as a Music Education Major.

Russell married Becky Kiewiet in August of 1969. This union produced three children, Ryan, Amy & Michael (Mike) as I refer to him. While working at different jobs which included band teaching, insurance sales and car sales, Russell always found time to camp, fish and detassel corn to help fund our annual Walt Disney trips every summer. In 1977, with the help of his father, my grandfather, Ardean, he built our home out in the country of Waterloo, Iowa on a half-acre of land.

Dad loved fishing, hunting and all the things that come with growing up on a farm. I recall several fishing trips, learning how to bait my own hook without gagging when the worm guts hit my fingers. The anticipation of the bite and listening to Dad calmly remind me to "reel him in — slowly, walk closer, pull back," all remain entrenched in my mind. Once the fish was on shore, Dad would often remind me step by step how to take the fish off the hook, where to hold the fish, especially the catfish so I wouldn't be poked. Always calm, always teaching.

In the summers, Dad made sure we attended Bible school, not only myself and my brothers, but also some of the neighborhood kids. I can recall kids piling in the back of the car to head to Zion Lutheran Church daily during summer vacation. It was always important to him that we had a relationship with Jesus. Weekends usually would include church on Sundays, followed by a 45-minute car ride to my grandparents' farm. These days included all the fun things a little girl could do on a farm. Playing with animals, shooting a BB gun, catching minnows in the creek or learning all the fishing skills I needed to catch the *biggest* fish.

So many fond memories, such as learning to drive Dad's car at the age of ten, yes ten. He was patient when I slammed on the brakes and we flew forward, he was patient when I forgot to slow down while turning and nearly rolled the car. His patience, was always followed by laughter.

Over the years Dad held many jobs, including tv repairman, band teacher and insurance salesman. For a number of years, I remember Dad working as a car salesman. This was a particularly *good* job because one of the benefits was driving a dealer car home each day. This made me feel pretty *cool*, being dropped off in a new car every day. He, too, was proud of the work he was doing.

Dad would contract acres of farmland each and every summer for our family to detassel corn. The money we made would ensure our annual *Disney World* trip. Oh, the memories of the drive to Florida, staying in the *Disney Campground* and the many memories left with me as a child at our favorite spot.

We, as a family, especially my dad and I, loved watching vacation movies, Clark Griswold taking the tribe across the country. We laughed over the years at how our family *Disney* trips often mirrored the Griswold's in so many ways. I will never forget going to the movie theater at the release of *Christmas Vacation*. Dad laughed from the beginning scene until the end scene without stopping, literally, non-stop, to the point I think he may have annoyed others in the theater. That didn't stop him, he laughed loudly and from his gut during the entire movie.

Although it wasn't a job to Dad, he could fix anything, including cars. His knack for figuring out how to fix an alternator or a heat pump on the side of the road were special gifts he possessed. I recall a time when he bought a vehicle with a blown motor. In only a few weeks he installed an entire new motor, and the car was headed down the highway. We often laugh when we think back to Dad in the garage working on a car—we could hear clearly if things were going well or a major challenge for him.

I spent my pre-teen and early teenage years as a swimmer. As a 12-year-old, I was ranked as the best swimmer in Iowa for my age group in two events, the 50- & 100-yard breaststroke. Dad would come to swim meets year-round, often having to follow my mom around to know when I was swimming my next event. He always had a book and highlighter with him, and there were times he had to be reminded I was up next, but he was always there. I recall getting ready to swim for the state championship. Dad laid out my towel and told me to lay flat and close my eyes. He walked me through my event from the starting block to the finish, while seeing myself win. Every single stroke, every single breath, he walked me through. He told me if I could see it, I could do it, and I saw myself winning both events. I did just that and became a state champion at the age of twelve.

It seemed as though Dad was always searching—searching for something. Reflecting, I see Dad laying on the couch with his *Bible* and an Anthony Robbins book, a highlighter and different color ink pens to make his notes. His *Bible* was marked up using anything from a colored pencil to a marker, note after note, joy after joy, or written quotes that he found inspirational throughout. Dad often spoke of "being a millionaire" by the time he was forty-five. He believed in manifesting these things and it was often Dad would willingly share this with others, it was no secret. Dad spent many hours laying with one leg stretched out over the back of the couch. Often he slept there, open book across his chest and highlighter painting his shirt.

In the summer of 1993, Dad began to voice some erratic concerns which he had never done before. I recall one evening, I went along with him to meet an old friend from his high school class for supper. This man was burly, wearing a black cowboy hat with a deep voice. At fourteen, I had little interest in their conversation, although I did pick up on a few things that night. The conversation was about the government, money owed to people and how Dad could play a huge roll in "bringing America back." I recall Dad's excitement for being asked to participate in such a great adventure. That night everything changed. The trajectory of events to follow were an endless nightmare for a daughter who loved her daddy with every-single-piece of my heart.

I wasn't an easy teenager (entering a sigh) and due to choices I had made around the age of fourteen, I was sent to live in a group home in Des Moines, Iowa. Dad and Mom would come visit me on weekends faithfully. Each weekend, things were becoming *different* with Dad. One visit, while walking to his car to grab supper, he showed me how he had turned his license plate upside down and said, "I own my car, not the State of Iowa." I was fourteen, maybe fifteen years old, and as any teenager, I laughed it off and continued to enjoy every second I had with my parents, which was a distraction from my current situation. My mom, not impressed, appeared to be angered by my dad's newfound interests.

On my parents 24th wedding anniversary, August 23, 1993, Dad left Mom a card with a necklace and ring on her desk at school.

After doing well in my group home, I was given overnight home weekend visits. The weekend of my parents' anniversary, I had a weekend planned at home, with the understanding I would need to return to Des Moines on Monday, along with Mom and Dad, so that we could have our next family therapy session. Dad was leaving on Saturday, heading to Minnesota for a *meeting* and said he would be returning on Monday, to join us for our session.

Mom and I drove Dad to meet a couple of people he was working with. A small, red, carry-on type of bag in hand, Dad got out of the car, hugged me, hugged Mom and said he would see us Monday. This was not unusual, as I understood, Dad had been going places frequently. In fact, he had just returned a couple weeks prior from a week-long trip to Jackson Hole, Wyoming for a *meeting*. My older brother, Ryan, went along with Dad on this trip. He had a passion for skiing, and there was no better place in his eyes, than Jackson Hole. Dad drove and Ryan joined him for the fifteen-hour drive. Ryan said Dad went to Jackson Hole one person and drove home a different person. I never was sure of the details to this statement; however, he was right in so many ways.

Monday came and our two-hour drive to Des Moines for our 4:00 p.m. therapy session was inching up on us, but no Dad. Cell phones were not a thing yet in 1993, unless like Dad, you had one of the car phones—a big bulky bag containing a big bulky phone, that cost an arm and a leg to talk on. Dad hardly used this phone, so there was no way to reach him. Mom and I jumped in the car and headed to Des Moines. We made our family therapy session; well Mom and I did. No Dad.

A day, two days, turned into a week. Nothing from Dad. My grandparents hadn't heard from him, and my concern became excruciating. I was alone in Des Moines, working on myself and wondered if he was even alive. During week two, my mom filed a missing person's report with our local police station. Week four, and no phone calls, nothing. Dad knew my schedule; he had worked around it for nearly a year to schedule visits.

I rode the bus to a mall in south Des Moines, faithfully, every single Friday after school. On this particular Friday, I got out of school, changed my clothes, and headed to the city bus. Walking into the mall I noticed right away a large group, maybe fifteen cowboys. Dad was a cowboy. I continued walking into the food court, where some of the cowboys were sitting and some standing in line at the Chinese restaurant. There he was. It was him. Black cowboy hat, an American flag shirt and cowboy boots. It was him. I ran, as fast as I could, my voice trembling, "DAD?" He turned, held his hands out and ran toward me. "DAD, what are you doing, where have you been?" I was yelling, with no care of who heard me. We reached each other and held on for what felt like dear life.

You're
Alive
Dad!!!!

In that brief moment, my hurt turned to anger, I pushed him back, "What are you doing? You've been missing, I've been so worried about you?" Dad responded with, "Sweet pea, I had to go undercover for the military and fight for our country. I want you to meet my new partner, my wife, Dana." Shock. What?

I couldn't look at the woman. Dad was always faithful, honoring the Lord, teaching others to honor the Lord. He honored marriage. *Who was this man? What had happened to my dad?* So many questions that would go unanswered. Despite the confusion, we were just happy to see each other. I was just happy to know he was alive. Now what?

Due to Dad's strange behavior, my counselor back at the group home had issued directives that my dad would only have supervised visits, until she determined what was going on. Dad could not be around me, so I devised a plan. I needed to be with him, I needed to stay in contact.

Dad drove me back to the home, and we planned a visit two weeks from that day, a Friday, but at the Subway near my highschool. He dropped me off around the corner and I was lost, yet thankful. I remember praying that night, asking Jesus what had happened to my dad, but more importantly thanking Jesus my dad was alive and ok.

I could not keep this from Mom, who was of course, as always, coming to visit me on Saturday, the very next day. Mom and I drove to a beautiful, familiar lake in North Des Moines. We got out, began to walk and I told her. It flowed out, I couldn't hold it in. "Mom, I saw Dad. He's ok." In pure disbelief, the tears fell, and she could hardly get the questions out fast enough. I told Mom everything, about the other woman, that he came to the mall because he knew that's where I would be, and that he was "undercover for the military."

My mom slowly sat down on a rock and continued to sob. I cried with her at that moment. I hurt for her. Twenty-four years of marriage, three children and a husband who left a ring and necklace on her desk at school just weeks prior. Now, to hear he was gone, broke her to pieces.

I was not allowed to see Dad. Mom shared the events with my counselor, who made it clear he was not to come to the home, and I was not to see him. I failed to tell them of our planned visit, and I wasn't going to share. I loved my dad; he was my best friend.

Two weeks took forever, but on that day I ran out of the front doors of Lincoln High school, through the parking lot to Subway and there he was. He was there. Black cowboy hat, black and white cowboy boots, and that huge smile that I loved so very much. We hugged, shared some tears, as he asked about my brothers and grandparents. I encouraged him to make contact, however, he said he could not speak to my brothers without going through a social worker, which he refused.

We went to another mall, and he bought me a long black leather trench coat from Wilsons Leather Store, which had been on my *want* list for some time. We didn't think of how I would get the coat back into the home without staff wondering where it came from. If I recall, I told them it belonged to a friend, but either way, I had my dream coat. Dad and I ate lunch, and he returned me to school late, missing a couple of classes. We planned on meeting again, the same way, the same time, but a little longer in between. One month.

I was discharged from the group home before that date arrived. Things were good. I had learned coping skills for some childhood traumas I had been dealing with. Home to Mom. I was not allowed to return to my old high school, so I was forced to go to a small town, south of Mom's. This was not for me. I hated it, and soon got the brilliant idea to contact Dad at a number I was given to see if I could go live with him.

I called. He was on his way. He drove from Seattle, Washington to get me, on his way to New York. I was a runaway and didn't look back. Dad picked me up in his brand-new van, and we made one stop. The Department of Human Services office. Dad had scheduled a visit with my little brother, Mike. There had been a court order that all visits were to be supervised with myself, and my younger brother, due to the erratic behaviors Dad was exhibiting.

Nobody knew I was in the van, in the parking lot.

Dad disappeared through the doors, and I laid in the back of the van, anxious and nervous at the same time, making sure I was not seen. Dad was in the building for about an hour. It wasn't until later on, I learned that as Mom was leaving the building after taking Mike into an office, the elevator doors opened and there was Dad. The excruciating pain she must have felt when their eyes met. The last time she saw him, he was her husband, and now a stranger. Dad got into the van, had some tears and we were on the highway to New York. Once we arrived in Jamestown, NY, Dad prepared for a seminar at a hotel conference center, and I walked around and went to the mall. Life seemed as though I was on an adventure to an unknown place. It was perfect.

I was now sixteen. I was now free.

1000 GIFTS FROM A 7 X 10

CHAPTER 2

City to City and Oh, the Adventures

Throughout 1994-1996, Dad was traveling across America, doing *law seminars* under the name, *America First*. My little knowledge of these seminars includes only that Dad was holding seminars sharing his newfound beliefs in a system that was unjust, and his new passion unfolded to share with the country.

My dad's common law wife, Dana, and her daughter, Ashley, were always traveling with us. Ashley and I became close and since she was only a year and a half younger than me, we spent a lot of time together. From what I understood, Ashley was not even her birth name, she went by this name because her mother supposedly never got her a social security number or birth certificate. I was never sure how truthful this was, but Dana in her intense, challenging demeanor, would share this with people often.

Ashley and I found adventures almost daily. There were trips to Philadelphia and nights experiencing iconic places like Philly Steaks or an afternoon in a helicopter flying through the city and down the Delaware River.

The moments of *normalcy* were frequent, very few interruptions that reminded me life was different. The lifestyle was in fact very different as I was not accustomed to things like shopping at King of Prussia mall on my 17th birthday with unlimited money, being able to buy what I wanted with no limitations. My favorite store at the time, Merry-Go-Round, earned a lot of my business on several different occasions.

Dad decided we should have a home—a "home base" as he would call it. A friend of his owned some townhomes and soon we had our place in Smithfield, North Carolina. A beautiful two-bedroom townhome very close to I-95. Ashley and I shared a room and Dad was able to purchase an entire law library book set to put in his new "office." Ashley and I loved this, we were able to venture out and have some normalcy instead of living from one hotel to another. We made friends, although we found it hard to describe our lifestyle with no school and frequent travel.

One week while in New York, Dad took us to the World Trade Center. Being from Iowa and now walking downtown New York, the skyscrapers surrounding me was an adventure in itself…oh how I just "took in" every sight, every smell, every moment. On the elevator, seeing over 100 different buttons to push for all the floors in the Trade Center was almost overwhelming, but Dad was standing next to me. He always made me feel safe despite whatever was going on around me. Once at the top the doors opened to a small gift shop with an escalator in the center. We rode that escalator to the observatory on the top of the Trade Center, and the sight was like nothing I had ever seen before. I recall looking off in every direction and making mental notes of the views. When we left, I had to stop in the gift shop and buy Angie, my very best friend, a key chain…it read ANGELA—ONE WORLD TRADE CENTER. Of course, I got the matching one with my name.

I recall going into a gun store one afternoon, just Dad and I. I had shot several different guns on my grandfather's farm growing up, I even went hunting with Dad on a few different occasions. This day was special because I was able to pick out a gun just for myself, and while searching through the cases in the store, a small pink Sig Sauer P228 stood out to me. Dad, of course, bought it. He was just as excited as I was, if not more. I never had time to shoot the gun, but I had it, it was mine.

Those treasured moments stand out, along with so many others. The moments with Dad when life seemed to be so very good, on a road with no destination with all kinds of excitement along the way.

Dad, and a team of others, specifically traveled the East Coast, setting up seminars to share the information he believed in with every fiber of his being. As a teenager, now living with Dad, Ashley and I were able to sit in and listen to these seminars from time to time. I find memories of these events bring a smile to my face. Dad was so happy, so driven and so eager to share. He felt important. I recall an event in Baltimore, Maryland, at a large church, where Dad walked in wearing his American flag cowboy shirt, ostrich skin boots, and black cowboy hat. With Neil Diamond's America playing loudly, Dad approached the front of the congregation, smiling and clapping while the crowd shared in his excitement. The song subsided and Dad began to speak with a heavy, eager voice that captivated all 2000 participants on that day. I recall looking around the room and thinking to myself, as a 16-year-old young woman, *Wow, my dad is famous.*

I was once told that you can always tell if you did a good job speaking at an event by how many people come up to you afterward and want to talk. This was true each and every time Dad spoke. So many people were interested in the things he had to say about injustice and how America was in *guerrilla warfare.*

1000 GIFTS FROM A 7 X 10

These seminars continued nearly every weekend—North Carolina, New York, Virginia. There was one particular seminar that stands out to me. Not everyone knows this, but it is part of my story and needs to be shared. This process of events, the Lord's plan had to happen for me to return home to Iowa, with my mother.

In Queens, New York, a weekend law seminar, similar to all other seminars, was being held at a Travelodge Hotel, right outside JFK airport. My step-sister, Ashley, and I provided a little help setting up the event room for the next seminar. I set up a coffee pot, set out some snacks and aligned the chairs.

On Friday evening, as the seminar began to attract guests, I sat off to the side, just to see how "famous" Dad would be in this event. I recall his theme song playing off in the distance, (*America*, Neil Diamond) and approximately 25-30 guests coming in, shaking hands with Dad and his team, and eventually everyone sitting down. Dad was always big on starting on time, and so that is what he did. Dad began speaking of the government, and all of the things he felt were wrong. At one point, I specifically recall him saying, "If you are undercover, police or FBI, I am so glad you are here. I hope you can learn something this weekend." It was at that moment, I thought to myself, why would they be here? I had so many questions on the reality of what was transpiring in Dad's life—and nobody to ask. I listened intently and then went on about my evening which usually consisted of Ashley and I swimming, watching movies, or taking a taxi to a mall.

The weekend was coming to an end, as was the law seminar. Packing up was a task shared by everyone who was working with Dad. It was always done so swiftly and efficiently. Dad asked me to go pull up his van so we could load our belongings, his speakers and all of the items he used in his seminars.

I walked out into the parking lot, free as a bird, even singing a little *Boyz II Men*, while the sun began to set behind JFK. While walking, I noticed a man, dressed in a bell boy uniform, walkie talkie in hand, following me. While I recall being somewhat nervous, I proceeded to unlock the van, hop in and head to the hotel entrance to load our things. While driving through the parking lot, that same bell boy was standing, still on his walkie talkie, watching me. I took note of the man on top of the hotel as well. Although it would seem as though I was unbothered, music playing and proceeding to the entrance, it flashed through my mind that something was amiss.

We loaded all our things and Dad spoke with one of his team members, who happened to be driving the same style of van, only his had green interior and ours was maroon. We pulled out at the same time. I was riding in the passenger seat, Dad driving, and my dad's wife Dana, another employee, Paula, and Ashley were all in the back. As we pulled out of the parking lot, I took note of the NYPD sitting off to the side, and so did Dad. He got on his CB radio, and began speaking with his partner, in the van in front of us. "Got a blue light special over here to the left!" It wasn't even thirty seconds after pulling out of the parking lot, blue and red lights were flashing, and one squad car pulled behind us and one behind Dad's partner. Dad pulled off to the side of the unlit, dark road directly behind the hotel. Dad and his partner were talking and reminding each other of the procedures when pulled over: Do not roll down your window, the definition of a license in Black's Law Dictionary, etc. Before I knew it, two NYPD officers were at Dad's window asking for his license and registration. Dad's window was rolled down an inch, van shut off so his Viper alarm system would shut everything down. Dad began to tell the officers he didn't have a license, nor did he need one because he had the constitutional right to travel upon the land. The conversation escalated quickly, and Dad shared he did not have the title to the vehicle, because he had the Certificate of Origin from the manufacturer, so he was going to be "on his way."

In no time, back-up came, Dad continued to converse with his partner, parked just thirty feet in front of us. Police were all around, Dad was adamant he would be "on his way" and the officers were not going to let him go without providing the requested information. A Sergeant, yelling at Dad through the window appeared, she yelled and demanded for Dad to "exit the vehicle." After about half an hour of refusing to exit, I noticed SWAT team members beginning to surround our vehicles. As a young, 16-year-old, while I knew this was not good, I had confidence in my dad's protection and knowledge in what he was doing. I felt safe. I felt nervous, but safe.

The SWAT team pulled the front of a semi cab up to the front of our van — and dropped a large bar made of metal onto our windshield. Dad told me several times to sit still, and this would be over soon. Conversations between Dad's wife and the other lady were becoming more and more agitated, although nobody ever said let's just get out of the van. In a split second the bar on our windshield turned to light, a heat light and the van began to get warm, then hot, then almost overwhelmingly hot. This is when I learned they were trying to *heat* us out of the van. I recall having to go to the bathroom, and Dad reminding me yet again, this would be over soon.

An officer outside of Dad's door again directed him to get out of the van, as it would be over 120 degrees and we would not be able to breathe. Dad stayed firm, and after about half an hour, the light shut off, the bar lifted off the windshield and the truck pulled away. Within seconds, the SWAT team got into place. I watched as officers in all black uniforms surrounded our van, and the van in front of us. An officer stood at the front of our van, over the driver's side headlight and leaned over on the hood pointing a rifle directly at me.

Dad asked me again to stay still, which I was finding more difficult to do, having to go to the bathroom. About an hour into this ordeal and here I am, in Queens, New York, on a back alley with a shotgun pointed in my face. *How did I get here? Will I see my mom again? Is my dad going to get us out of this, and if so, how?*

More SWAT members ran up to Dad's window, placed three or four small suction cups to the window, and I heard a loud shatter as the window broke in millions of pieces. I saw arms reaching in through Dad's window as they opened the door and pulled him out of his seat and immediately to the ground. I was frozen, I now realized there were officers at my door sticking the same suction cups to my window. As I unconsciously opened my door, I was pulled by my hair, shirt and leg and thrown to the ground. As I lay with my face in gravel, I began to cry. I didn't understand, I didn't know what to do. The officers handcuffed me, picked me up and walked me over to the squad car as I watched them pulling out our purses, and dumping them onto the trunk of a squad car.

Placed in the back seat of a squad car with no understanding of what was about to transpire, I watched out the window as we pulled away, seeing my Dad being placed in another car. The drive from the scene to our destination, sticks in my brain like it was yesterday.

I was now in Times Square, a place I was hoping to see while visiting New York, however, not in the back of a police car. The lights, my tears and confusion. *Where am I going? What did I do? How will I get home?* We ended up at a precinct in Brooklyn and were placed in a single cell in the back of an office—chipped paint, a light blue with yellow tint from stains of aging. Myself, my 14-year-old half-sister, Dad's wife and a friend from his team. All females, uncuffed and shoved into this small cell, with the usual bars and one small bench. We sat on the floor, and then Dad and the male driver of the other van were brought in, set in a chair, and cuffed to the seat. The smell of sweat and filth was horrid. Officers were coming in and out and eventually the angry sergeant came in. She was eager to inform us we were all going away for a while after finding Dad's loaded .357 and 350 rounds of hollow-point bullets in the bag. She continued to question Dad, "What are you planning on using those bullets for Mr. Landers?"

Dad would always respond to her matter of fact, "What else is in the bag, why do you keep forgetting that? What else? There is also a *Bible* in the bag ma'am!"

I sat, in the corner, knees pulled to my chest watching these interactions, feeling crushed and confused.

After about twelve hours in this holding cell, a couple of officers came into the room and said they were taking the males, Dad and his friend, the driver of the other van, and before I knew it he was gone.

There I was, sixteen years old and scared. *Now what happens? Can I call my mom?* Shortly after Dad was taken, three female officers came and said it was time to get on the bus. *The bus? What bus? Where am I going?*

We were taken down dark hallways with flickering lights to a sally port where I saw *the bus*. A white bus with blue and orange stripes on the side, the same bus I saw the week prior while watching a new episode of *Lock Up-Rikers Island*. *This couldn't be true, so where were they taking me?*

Ashley and I were handcuffed to each other and so were Dad's wife and co-worker. We sat in the front seat, and a couple of other inmates on the bus were questioning us, asking who we were, making comments about our clothing, jewelry, and stating, "Nobody goes to Rikers looking like you guys."

My heart sank. *Was I going to Rikers Island? Will they let me call my mom? Where is my dad, Rikers?* The bus pulled off and before I knew it I watched as we turned onto a long road surrounded by water to one of the scariest places I had ever seen in my life. Barbed wire, dogs, people yelling as we exited the bus, still handcuffed together. Once in this building, I noted it looked like a large horseshoe with cells, some small, some very large. I felt a sense of sadness for the women, some of the cells so full there was nowhere to sit. There was yelling, arguing, crying and emptiness in the eyes of so many I made eye contact with. We were taken to an empty, smaller cell and the gate swinging door closed loudly. This was really happening.

A young officer came to our cell and began asking questions of my stepmother. She wanted to know what a family that *looked like us* was doing in Rikers Island. She was forward, yet curious as to who we were. She asked several times how old Ashley was, and my stepmother would respond with a fake age, as she did not want Ashley to be taken to a juvenile facility. At one point, she asked us, "Who are you guys? You're white supremacist?"

Within a short time, a male Sergeant came to our cell and stood on the other side of the gray metal bars, he looked at us with questions in his eyes and began asking them, "Who are you, I have worked at Rikers Island for seventeen years and I have never seen on someone's intake papers that they were white supremacist and KKK, you just won't make it in here."

My stepmother began to spout out at the officer, "My husband is a common law judge, and someone is trying to kill us." While I sat and listened to this conversation, my mind began to wander. *How did I get here? Is this really happening? Where is my dad?*

Hours passed, while we sat in this cell, and we were eventually herded to a room in the back of the building. This room consisted of three open showers, and three doctor office exam tables. We were ordered to strip, completely strip. Both male and female officers yelled directives, "Strip, step in the shower, two minutes, use the lice shampoo, rinse and get out!"

Every cell in my being was terror-stricken, my breath became shallow, and I froze in my steps. Although able to follow instructions, I became numb, standing in the shower using the lice shampoo, I questioned all of the *whys* to the entire event transpiring. Once out of the shower, we were directed to the exam table, where a man dressed in a white doctor coat, directed me to lay back on the table, put my feet in the stirrups, nothing to cover up with, my 16-year-old body frozen to the core. The man performed a cavity search, and I was directed to get dressed and stand against the white brick wall. Tears fell, both from my eyes and internally if that makes any sense. As I waited for the next directive, Ashley and the others completed the tasks, and we were then returned to our cell.

The male sergeant returned to our cell and made it very clear that we would not survive in the general population. It had already spread that there was a family of *white supremacists* in the intake area — we didn't have a chance. This man informed us that because of the danger we were in, he would be putting us in protective custody, a special unit.

The frustration I felt of being called a racist and KKK member burned my heart, literally. Why were these people saying these things? Was it the Sergeant who yelled at us that put this on our intake papers? Someone actually put this on our intake papers? Do they not know our closest friends are of different races?

We were escorted down endless hallways, Correctional Officers (CO's) went ahead of us, behind us and on both sides as we walked and followed the black line on the floor. Women walking down the halls were yelling and staring at us. My frightened body was frozen, although I took step after step. We came to a black metal door, the loud keys of the CO unlocked the door, and we entered a two story, open room and were greeted with a CO sitting in a chair. The COs exchanged some words and we were directed to stand in a line against the wall.

The CO stood from her chair and handed us a sheet and a comb. We later found out we were not given the other necessities, no toothbrush, no cup for drinks, no top sheet or blanket. We were directed upstairs to put our things in our cells, and instructed we would have an hour before we were required to return to our cells for the night. I recall coming out of my cell and waiting for Ashley and the others, while so many other women stared at us with aggressive looks as well as almost a look of disbelief.

Eventually we all walked downstairs to the living area which consisted of plastic chairs around tables, maybe five of them. We sat together at a table, tired, stressed, afraid and somewhat in shock about all of the events that had occurred over the last twenty-four hours. It was at this time, a woman, probably 6'4", came from behind me, leaned down and whispered in my ear, "Mmmmm white girls turn me on."

I turned to look at her, masculine build, goatee and a flat top haircut. My step-mother immediately interceded and began a conversation with the woman to distract her original thoughts.

My stepmother was good at this, good at deflecting conversations and getting others to believe things that may or may not be true. The woman too asked questions about who we were, and why would the CO sitting in the doorway tell her to come "beat our ass."

Only a short time went by, and we knew the woman's story, and she knew ours. She was in Rikers for killing her girlfriend, which she claimed was self-defense. Either way, I could not believe the things I was hearing, the environment I was in and the events that were transpiring. Soon, we made several *friends* and my stepmother had everyone believing her off-the-wall stories of being set up, her husband (Dad) was a common law judge, and even that she would be helping them all get out of prison. The lights flickered — bed time. To our cells.

I walked up the stairs, hugged my sister, and walked into my cell as it closed loudly behind me. This was real. This was very real. I am in a cell in Rikers Island. The walls, painted a light gray, almost white, paint chipped everywhere, a small bed against the wall, a small metal sink and a toilet. I laid my sheet over my bed as tears fell. Now I am frightened. My breath became shallow as I laid on my bed — the stiffness to the air and the sound of nothing. Nothing. No window, no blanket, no toothbrush. Stillness.

I rocked myself to sleep, as I often did, crying, really crying, curled in a ball. A loud noise woke me the next morning. I remember this vividly, because waking up to the reality of being in a cell still scares me to this day. I was a child, a teenager, in a cell, alone. My cell door opened, and I walked out to Ashley walking toward me with tears in her eyes. We walked downstairs to the tables and sat as they passed out trays of breakfast, or so-called breakfast. A piece of toast, a slice of cheese and maybe grits, I am still unsure. This was the first time we realized in order to drink anything, you had to have your green cup — which we didn't receive when we were put into protective custody. We asked, nobody would give us one.

Ashley and I were able to *borrow* one from our new friends and the stories of who we were and conversations about helping others get out continued throughout the day, until count time, and then again throughout the evening, until count time, and more conversations until lights out.

On Wednesday, (we had been here since Monday, arrested on Sunday) a Chaplain from the prison came to see us. We shared our horrific battle of coming into the prison, being labeled, and the treatment from the guards — not giving us basic necessities. She was an older woman, maybe in her seventies. She listened and said she would try to help. She was able to schedule a phone call between my dad and my stepmother. This phone call took place that evening somewhere outside of the protective custody unit.

When she returned from the call she said Dad was at a county jail in Queens and was ok. He was working on sending visitors up to us, and to let us know we would be getting out very soon. She also mentioned, "Amy, your dad said to tell you he loves you too." Oh, my heart, my dad is ok, and he is thinking of me. In my mind I mumbled, "I love you too Dad."

On Thursday morning we were told to line up, as we had a visit. A visit? *Who knew we were here?* We walked the black line with guards all around us. Inmates were also walking the hall, glaring and yelling things at us as we walked by. We got to a cell and were told to sit there until we were brought into the visiting room. We sat. I was along the wall, knees pulled to my chest, wearing the same clothes I came into Rikers in three days prior. My hunter green *Karl Kani* shirt, red *Kani* jeans and of course my *Timberland* boots that I loved so so so much. Inmates were on the other side of the bars yelling things at us, even reaching between the bars at one point. I sat and stared at them, wanting so badly to tell them who we really were and that we were not a family of white supremacists. I didn't, I just stared.

Soon, a guard came to get us, and we went into a small room. Here we were told to undress, all the way down to nothing. Again, humiliated and scared, I did as I was told. I didn't understand but followed the directions only to turn around and get dressed again. We were then taken into a room with lots of people, sitting in chairs and as I was getting used to, staring. Everyone was staring. Then from across the room I saw two familiar faces, friends of my dad's, Eric & Deanna. They lived in New York and even had us over for dinner while we were there a few months prior. Oh, how I could feel the blood rush through my body from the tip of my head to the souls of my feet. Deanna hugged me first, she held me, she wiped my tears and kissed my forehead. Eric followed suit…and we sat at the table we were assigned. I sat, holding Deanna's hand throughout the entire visit. Conversations and the staring turned from almost angry stares to, who are these people and why were we spreading this false rumor, or at least that was the impression I was feeling. Eric & Deanna were African American, beautiful people, both inside and out. Dad had reached them from the jail he was in, and they insisted on coming to check on us. And there they were. The visit was short, but they assured us that they, and others, were doing everything they could to get us out. Tears fell, my stomach in knots, I hugged them goodbye as the visit ended and off they went.

Things changed after that visit. I felt even the guards had somehow been told of our visit and people now even wanted to be around us more on our unit.

One lady, a mother, probably in her late twenties, would sit with us often. I only recall her beauty, despite the obvious, no makeup or hair products. I remember her story: she murdered her boyfriend when he and his *side* girlfriend came into her home. She said there was no self-defense law in New York and so they were charging her with murder, even though he came into her home and had a knife. That was her story, I don't know how true, but it's what she told us. My heart hurt for her, and I was called to pray for her. I did, I listened to the Lord and asked her if I could, to which she agreed. She wept, I wept. She hugged me and I hugged her. I do not recall her name, but I have thought of her more than once over the last thirty years.

The days were long, the same routine, the same stories, the same food. Saturday morning, we were again called to the front of the unit. We were leaving, going to court. I found this odd because it was Saturday. We were taken through the halls, to the sally port and put back on that bus with the blue and orange stripes, down the road surrounded by water and taken to the courthouse. Once inside, we were put in a holding cell, and there we waited. The thoughts running through my mind only consisted of, will I get out of here or will I be back on the bus to Rikers? How much time will they give me? I sat and sat and eventually was escorted to a very large courtroom and the first thing I saw was Dad. *Daddy, oh Daddy — do you know where I have been?*

We were taken to the front of the courtroom and stood in front of over a hundred of my dad's friends. I recall so many officers standing around the perimeter of the room. The judge began to speak and read off our charges. My thoughts were racing. I am being charged with possession of a gun, a class D felony. The judge began to speak and questioned who my sister was and more importantly, how old she was. The judge ordered for her to be released immediately. I turned and watched her walk into the courtroom gallery. I was up next, my heart pounding as the district attorney noted, "Your honor, Amy is a missing person out of Iowa. We should find out from Iowa the cause of the missing person report."

My dad immediately jumped into the conversation and said, "How can she be missing, she is right here?"

The judge sternly said, "In the state of New York, Amy is an adult, and we will set her bond at $2,500 cash only."

I stood in silence. The judge went down the line, my step-mother, and my dad's friend $5,000 cash only and then to my dad. The judge seemed angry and set his bail at $25,000 cash or security. My heart sank and I felt at that moment Dad would not be able to get out. We were escorted back to the same holding cell as when we arrived. There I sat, tears fell, I thought to myself nobody would spend $2,500 to get me released. At that moment, a guard came and told me I was being released. Shortly after, my step-mother and Dad's friend were released as well.

I ran out after being processed. I found my sister along with Eric & Deanna, and so many others. I walked out of the doors of the courthouse and saw a payphone. I knew I had to call my mom and my best friend, Angie, back home. *Did they know where I had been? Were they looking for me?* I believe I made a collect call home, Mom answered. My first words to her were, "You know where I've been don't you?" Mom said she didn't know and so I began to cry and tell her I had been in Rikers Island, and I wanted to come home. Mom could be trusted. Her stability, her honesty, her indomitable courage, would ensure I could slowly "go in the right direction" no matter the circumstances.

Mom was in disbelief, and I shared a snippet of the prior week's events with her. I cried telling her Dad was not out and I was so worried he wouldn't be getting out. She assured me, as she always did, "everything will be ok, Amy." She asked that I keep in contact, and she would see what she could do to get me home.

My next call was to my best friend, Angie, my lifelong best friend. She accepted my call and there were tears, laughter and the usual, "Come home Amy, I miss you" conversation. I assured her my plans were to head home, if and only if I could get Dad out and he didn't run away with me to Florida. Yes this was my hope at that moment, my new goal was to get Dad to leave this group and run away with me, take his money and start over.

I was now afraid for him to my core. My heart felt a physical pain, thinking of him still behind bars in such horrific circumstances.

Some of Dad's followers assured me they would do whatever it took to get him out, however it would take a few days.

We stayed with Eric & Deanna for a few days in Queens. Life wasn't the same, my anxiety seemed to always be on high alert. Dad was finally released a few days later; I learned that someone put up their home for him to get out. We were then on the road back to our townhome in North Carolina. I knew I had to leave Dad. I needed to go back home to Iowa and move on with my life. I was now seventeen and it was time. My fear of staying with Dad and being in a situation like I had just been in was too dreadful to think of. I would have to find a time to discuss my concerns with Dad. I knew he would understand, or would he?

I contacted my mom and came up with a plan. She had been in contact with local DHS (Department of Human Services) workers who told her the State of Iowa would use interstate compact monies to buy me a ticket home. After several calls we had a plan. I decided not to tell Dad my plan. I didn't want to hurt him, but I was afraid, afraid of returning to prison or the unknown of Dad's lifestyle.

In September of 1994, I was able to execute my plan to return to Iowa. With the help of two amazing social workers, Toni and Robert, along my mother, I would be picked up by an officer at 7:00 p.m. while walking to Blockbuster video. In order to confuse others, I even planned to use my fake name, Sheila, so that Ashley wouldn't pick up on my plan.

At 6:45 p.m. I told Ashley I was walking to the video store, and of course, she was coming along. I went to Dad, kissed him, hugged him and even sat on his lap for a second. We laughed and I looked into his eyes, knowing my plan was transpiring in the next thirty minutes.

I experienced much anticipatory grief in this moment, the unknown of what our futures held. Would Dad be part of it if I chose to leave? My mind definitely knew the uncertainty of Dad's future—so yes, I had to go, but my heart felt the heaviest it's ever felt. I touched his hand, smiling but holding back the threatening tears. I squeezed his hand three times, then turned toward the door with nothing but my purse and the clothes on my back. As I got to the door I turned one more time and blew Dad a kiss as he sat behind his new "lawyer" like desk. I had no clue when I would ever see him again.

While walking as normal teenage girls, we sang, danced, and continued our normal path to Blockbuster Video. About five minutes into our walk, a squad car pulled up next to us, the officer got out of the car and came directly to me. Ashley became defensive, even argumentative. I told the officer my name was Sheila, and he knew the plan, and went along with it. He said, "You look just like Amy, a missing person out of Iowa." I laughed and said no several times. Finally, he made it clear that I was in fact Amy Landers, and he would be taking me downtown.

Ashley took off running and yelled, "I'm going to get Dad!" I got into the squad car and was driven to the Smithfield police station. I was taken to the back and questioned about what I was doing in North Carolina. I didn't feel I needed to answer questions, I just wanted my airline ticket home.

About fifteen minutes had passed and I could hear Dad. He was in the entry of the station, asking for me, "Where is she, she is my daughter?" Stern and angry. While I do not know how, or what was said, Dad left. The officers said I would have to go to a youth shelter while waiting for my ticket. I was angry and told them I would not go to a shelter. I wanted to leave and was told I had an airline ticket.

They allowed me to call Mom, and she said it would take a day or two to get the ticket. I refused. I was ready to walk out of the station when an officer said he would get me a hotel room for the night and pick me up the next day and take me to the airport. I agreed and they took me to a log cabin hotel, after stopping to purchase some snacks for me at a convenience store. Oddly enough, I had stayed in this hotel, right off I-95, with Dad when we were looking for a place to live.

More than once I had been here, and the thought of leaving Dad flooded my heart again. I heard his voice, I heard him pleading with the officers to let me go, my heart sank in my chest as tears fell. I thought of all the events in New York and thought of the future for Dad. *How did he change from a normal dad, husband, son, into a man who was being followed by the FBI and going to jail? How did he change so much?* I was alone in this hotel and heartbroken.

The next morning, an officer came to my room, told me it was time to go, and drove me to the Raleigh-Durham airport. He dropped me off and told me I could make a collect call to the number he was handing me if I needed to. He directed me to the ticket counter. There was no ticket.

I called Mom, she didn't know and told me she would be reaching out to Toni and to call her back. Morning turned to afternoon and afternoon turned to evening. I was hungry, without money, I was dirty, without clothing or hygiene items. All of the clothes, makeup, hair products, everything was at Dad's. *Was he angry with me? Does he know I set all of this up to go back home?*

I was informed I would not receive my ticket until right before my flight which would most likely be the next day. I broke down and curled up into a ball in the nearest chair. I knew I had one person who would help me, who would take care of me. Dad. I went to the payphone and called. He answered the phone and accepted my collect call.

"Dad, I'm at the airport, can you bring me some money so I can eat and bring me a bag of my stuff?" His voice was hurt, and hollow. He asked if this was my plan, and I told him the truth. He didn't understand and asked if I would stay. It took everything I had to tell him I could not stay for fear of everything that was happening, and he agreed to bring me some of my stuff.

It was dark outside and while sitting in front of the airport, I saw Dad pull in. He was not alone—his wife and the friend who drove the other van were with him. He got out of the van and hugged me while we both cried. I can still smell the leather from his black cowboy hat, black leather cowboy feathered coat, and gray cowboy boots. He said my bag was in the back of the van and that I could climb in and get it. I felt strange about this, and my step-mother rudely told me to get it myself or I wouldn't get it. Dad looked strange, with a sad face and I told him I wasn't getting in the van, and so he did. My step-mother and Dad's friend were making comments, and I asked Dad to get me a room at the hotel across the street so I could shower and sleep, as my flight wouldn't be coming until the next day. He agreed and walked with me to the hotel, with his friend following behind us. I reached out and grabbed his hand, he squeezed it three times, which we had done since I was a little girl, which meant, I love you.

Through tears, I stopped him in the path, turned to him and looked him in his eyes. My whole life I could get Dad to do what I wanted; he found it very hard to tell me no.

"Dad, come with me, let's just go. Bring your money, leave everything, let's go Dad, let's go to Florida and start over. Dad I am afraid for you, you're going to go to prison, and I cannot live with that."

He grabbed my face with both of his hands and said, "I can't do that baby, I have to fight for our country. You can stay with me. You don't have to go."

In that moment, my heart, my best friend, my daddy, chose to fight for the country instead of for me. I was broken. I cried, and cried, and cried some more as we finished our walk to the hotel. Dad's friend checked me in, while I stood in the lobby hugging my daddy, still crying. Dad was crying. I was handed my room key, room 331 if I recall and Dad said, "I got to go, I love you sweet pea." Again, I tried to get him to stay with me, and he pulled out $200 and handed it to me. Dad hugged and squeezed me again as he said, "I will see you soon, okay," then turned and walked away. I will never forget as he walked out the door. I stood crying as he turned to look at me with tears in his eyes as he left.

I took the elevator to my room and collapsed on the bed, as I fell asleep crying, yet again.

The next morning, I awoke, and went through my bag. Odds and ends, unmatching clothes, but I had clothes, some makeup and was able to make myself presentable. I checked out of the hotel and walked back over to the airport. I recall looking around, just to see if maybe Dad changed his mind. He didn't, he wasn't there.

My airline ticket was there and soon I was landing at my hometown airport in Waterloo, Iowa. As I exited the plane, I could see my faithful mother, and younger brother, Mike, in the window.

I was home.

CHAPTER 3

The Standoff

During my first month back home in Iowa, I spoke with Dad frequently. I often inquired about what he was doing. My curiosity followed up with questions saved me from losing myself in the *what ifs*. My mom hired her attorney to handle my case in New York, considering I still had a Class C felony for possession of Dad's gun and bullets. Through a lot of phone calls, an agreement was made to have me return to New York to testify against Dad, and in return all my charges would be dismissed. My attorney made it clear, we must have it in writing, if I participated and spoke with the Grand Jury I would no longer have charges.

Next thing I knew, my mom, brothers and I were on a plane to Queens, New York. I spent an entire day being asked question after question about the people my Dad was around, about conversations I may have heard and specifics about locations we had been. I sat on the stand in tears and shared the little bits of information I had. This was torture in so many ways, I often found myself questioning my own memory and at one point, sat with my head down in front of strangers, as tears fell. I was allowed to retrieve some of my things from the storage room at the courthouse—my bag with clothes, Dad's Bible and a few odds and ends.

That was it. My charges were dropped, and we went back home to Iowa.

Life was happening, I had my first son, Alex—my pride, joy and reason to succeed in life. A little boy with curly blond hair and blue eyes. Dad would often ask for pictures of him and speak with him during our phone calls.

On a bright and sunny day, my best friend, Angie, and I decided to take our babies to a local park to swim. Little did I know, the New York incident would flare up yet again. While driving to the lake, a State Patrol pulled us over. Angie was driving, I was in the passenger seat, and our children in the back seat. The officer came to the passenger side door and asked me to step out of the car, to which I complied. He began to handcuff me and tell me I had a warrant out of New York, despite my pleas with him, that all of that had been dismissed. I was taken down to the station and immediately called my mom. I was placed in a holding cell, in my swimming suit—more tears. Mom immediately spoke with our attorney who handled my case. If I recall, he was at the jail within five minutes, or what seemed very quickly. He presented the documentation that my charges were in fact dismissed, and after review by a judge, I was released. I was sure to let Dad know of this event, and he apologized yet again, a deep, heartfelt apology for the craziness that still resulted from the New York events.

A calendar event I'll never forget occurred in April of 1996. On a phone call with Dad, he spoke of Montana and that he would be there for a little while. He gave me a phone number to reach him, and I wrote in down and tucked it away in my billfold. While at Angie's a couple of days later, I was sitting in the burgundy swivel chair in the living room while Angie laid on the couch. In the background, the news was on.

THE STANDOFF

During our conversation I vaguely overheard the news story, a standoff had begun in Montana with a radical anti-government group. My mind went back and forth quickly like a light turning on and off. *Could that be Dad? Am I right, was the phone number he gave me somewhere in Montana? I sat quietly, thinking if it was him, what would happen?* I recalled other standoffs that did not have happy endings, such as Waco and Ruby Ridge. I mentioned to Angie about my most recent call with Dad and that he had given me a phone number in Montana if I needed to reach him. I will never forget the look on her face, it was like she already knew this story on the news did in fact involve my dad.

(It should be noted here — these are only the events I knew, I lived, I perceived. This is not the story of the Montana Freemen.)

I went to Mom's house to ask if she had heard anything. She had not and had not yet heard of a standoff in Montana. When I shared the phone number and described the group to her, she said she hoped not and suggested I should try to call the number. I did. There was no answer.

The next day brought on what would be one of the hardest days of my life. Mom called me with desperation in her voice and asked me to come over right away. When I pulled into the driveway I was met with a vehicle that I did not recognize, and as I walked in the back door, voices I had never heard. When I came into the living room, there were two men, dressed in dark blue, and I could clearly see FBI on their jackets. I knew already. They did not have to say a word. I sat down with my hands clenched together, trying to focus on my breathing, my heart pounding. *Is he dead? What happened? Why are you at my mom's?* So many thoughts, so many emotions, feelings. *Breathe Amy, breathe.*

One of the agents began to speak and although a lot of what

he was saying was mumbled as it processed through my ears to my brain, I did hear Montana, standoff, dangerous, and sorry. A nightmare was happening, right in front of me, a nightmare I never fathomed could exist. It was starting, and my dad was a key player in the nightmare while I was forced to stand on the sidelines. Dad had always taught me to talk to my Father when things were out of my control, which I did in that moment.

The agents asked me several questions because of my frequent contact with Dad, and the fact I lived with him for a while. They wanted the phone number Dad gave me, and with hesitation I gave it to them. My little brother, a young teenager at the time, looked the men in the face and said, "Are you going to shoot my dad?" I needed to hear the response to the question, I needed to know, and I was so glad he asked the question, although I was burning up inside in fear of the answer I would receive. One of the agents told us they didn't want to shoot anyone, but if Dad or others in the standoff started to shoot at them, they would have no choice.

Was I really hearing this? My dad was not violent, had never been violent, how could this conversation be happening, here in Mom's living room? I jumped in and made it clear to the agents, "My Dad loves the Lord, he has strange beliefs, yes he does, but he will not hurt anyone. ANYONE. I know my dad better than anyone and his heart would never allow him to hurt anyone. He may talk a big game, he IS very intelligent, please just hear what he has to say and end this peacefully." I even asked if I could go in. Although that was discussed it was decided for my safety I would not be allowed to go to Montana.

Days went on, the major news channels would give hourly updates on the standoff. "The Montana Freemen are still held up on a 960-acre ranch and are refusing to come out." I would often sit and watch the news, flipping between channels and hitting

THE STANDOFF

record on the VCR every time the story was on. Sometimes there was video of people in the standoff going to the end of the two-mile-long driveway to meet with agents, and I could see Dad. He would always have his cowboy hat on and would even shake hands with others. This was the dad I knew; I will never believe he had any intent to hurt anyone. Again, I knew him best.

One evening, Dateline NBC was airing a special on The Montana Freemen standoff. I made sure I was recording and watched as those in the standoff were called radicals, and even violent, which I absolutely knew not to be true, at least my dad. Dad was quoted often, and there were even audio recordings playing of Dad in heated discussions with agents.

I learned my sister, Ashley, was in the standoff. I was afraid for her and even felt sorry for her. The media shared there were other children with their parents in the standoff. I believe a total of twenty-three people were held up on this 960- acre ranch, and my understanding was this was all over unpaid taxes of the owner of the ranch. There were approximately seven homes on this land, a lake and even generators to last for quite some time.

Daily, I watched from afar. About fifty days into the standoff, the same FBI agents were again at Mom's. We were asked to film a video and ask Dad to come out of the standoff. The agent, with his large video camera recorded us as we each pleaded with Dad to come out. Mom made a sign and taped it to Alex's stroller, reading *Grandpa please come out, I want to meet you*. Alex in his stroller, sign on the front smiling, while I stood in my Mom's driveway, reminding Dad of just who was in control and to please come out. There wasn't a moment when tears were not falling, and the pit of my stomach in knots, that hadn't gone away since the first day I became aware of the standoff. "Daddy, please come out, Alex wants to meet you!"

The tape was eventually taken into the standoff, and Dad had watched it. He later told me we looked like movie stars and seeing Alex touched every cell in his body. Days went on, the news continued to share live streams from up to two miles away, zoomed in on the ranch. Helicopters, squad cars, and regular cars sat in the distance. There was sometimes close-up video of some of the Freeman, walking the perimeter, cowboy hats on and a rifle on their shoulders. Some rode horses through the night, some walked alongside. Soon, the electricity had been cut to the ranch, however the generators kicked in and they still had light.

One video captured one of the men, which was possibly Dad hanging an upside-down flag on a flagpole, and I knew from living with Dad, that this meant *America was under siege.*

I didn't understand any of this. Dad had always been an average, normal dad, husband, son, and friend. Often those closest to my family would phone to ask so many questions that we didn't have answers for.

Dad's parents had to live through this. Days of news, the front page of the newspapers, oh the heartbreak my grandmother felt. My grandfather, a tall man, 6'4, was crushed. His only son, making headlines for having a standoff with the government. I could only imagine their pain.

I recall walking into a local grocery store one day, the old newspaper stand stood out front of the store, and as I walked by, *Local Waterloo Man Leads Montana Freemen* and a large picture of the man I resemble in so many ways, the man who has always been my best friend, who taught me to drive, to fish, and who Jesus was. *Who was that man on the front page of the paper?* When these thoughts went through my mind, nobody, and I mean nobody could begin to understand the confusion, the emptiness I felt, each and every day.

THE STANDOFF

There were some others from past standoffs, going in to "talk the group out of the holdup," people like Dad's friend, Randy Weaver. The only thing I knew about Randy was he was in some type of standoff like Dad's in Ruby Ridge, and I knew his family had been killed. I was terrified this would happen to Dad.

There were statements made one evening by President Bill Clinton, I caught the very end and recall thinking to myself, *Wow, this is a really big deal, the President is talking about Dad!* There were attorney generals giving statements on *Breaking News*. So much happening, and as a young woman, I had no idea how or where to feel the emotions that were running like wildfire through my brain, through my heart. With all of that, I just…didn't…want…Dad…to…die. To…be shot. I could not live with this.

I learned through conversations with some of Dad's friends during this time, that my stepmother had known these people in Montana, and they had asked her and Dad to come help them because their ranch was being foreclosed on for unpaid taxes. **This wasn't even Dad's idea.** This wasn't even his idea; do you know how many times that went through my head? Can you imagine the anger I felt inside? I knew Dad had a choice, but it was like he was driven by this woman, it was her idea, her friends, and her that led him to Montana. This hurt, this made me angry and so very disgusted with her as a person. We already had our issues when I was living with them. She was angry, she was mean, she was forceful, and I caught her in so many lies.

There was word the standoff was possibly coming to an end. The media would say they had learned that the Freemen were coming to a resolution with the FBI. Oh, this gave my heart joy. Will Dad go to prison? *Will Dad be free since he is coming out?* So many questions every hour of every day.

Breaking news: June 14, 1996.

The Freemen were coming out of the standoff. Some agreement had been reached between them and the FBI. I was shaking, I was pacing, I was so afraid. I sat directly in front of Mom's television. I was glued. Literally. With the VHS player recording each and every major news channel, I waited. I watched and then, there was Dad's motorhome going down the long, two-mile driveway, slowly. The FBI had agents everywhere, with two blue vans parked at the spot where Dad would come down daily to meet with them. It seemed as if that drive took hours. *What was Dad thinking, was he afraid? How will this end?*

Lord, protect my daddy, Lord go before him. Lord hear my prayer. I remember praying—praying as Dad had taught me to do when I was afraid. Lord be near. Lord touch.

The motorhome came to a stop. Nothing. No movement. One minute seemed like eternity. Two minutes, seemed like eternity times ten. Five minutes, the **Breaking News** hadn't even gone to a commercial. The door opened. People started to come out and walk toward the agents. There he was. There was my daddy. Black cowboy hat, his Mickey Mouse leather coat. He was walking toward the agents. It was ending, or was it beginning?

Dad stood talking, and then he turned around and was handcuffed, right on live TV. The others were handcuffed, and he was escorted to one of those blue vans. I could clearly see him with the sunlight hitting the side of the van. His hat made his silhouette noticeable. *Oh, my heart, what is next?*

It's over.

No, it has just begun.

CHAPTER 4

The County Jails

Dad was now in the Yellowstone County Jail in Billings, Montana, awaiting his court hearings. I never attended a hearing. I couldn't bear to watch, or listen. During this time, he was flown to North Carolina for sentencing on bank fraud and mail fraud charges and had been named on a superseding indictment out of the Eastern District of North Carolina in July of 1996.

There were plenty of newspaper articles to follow during these times, and plenty of phone calls from Dad. I vaguely remember my first collect call from him a few days after the end of the standoff. Many tears from us both, and he shared he had been stripped down to his undershorts and placed in a concrete room with no bedding. He was angry more than anything, more frustrated than he had been in a very long time. My heart hurt for him. He spoke of refusing to sign anything for the officers, which he feared was going to cause some sort of problem. *Why don't you sign anything Dad? Why make things worse?* He didn't believe in signing anything, anything at all. This call was tough.

Another call, maybe a month later, Dad shared of placement in 23-hour lock down due to his refusal to sign papers, no commissary, and he felt like the little bit of food he was getting was starving him. In my notes, (I took many) he shared of the small veggie soup, noting it didn't even cover the bottom of the bowl was all he had in a 24-hour period. He was refusing counsel, refusing to cooperate.

In a letter from Dad in September of 1996, nearly four months after the standoff ended, he told me he was named on a superseding indictment out of North Carolina and would be going there for court. He mentioned that he demanded an extradition hearing, however, that was denied. He talked of this incident often, it hurt him. It hurt me. He said US Marshals came in and drug him out of his cell, slammed his face on a concrete wall, which created a wound in his forehead, where blood ran down the wall and down his face. He was chained and taken to an airplane at the Billings airport and flown to Will Rogers Airport in Oklahoma. The following day he was flown to Raleigh-Durham, North Carolina. Dad had court here. He was angry, he truly believed he could win this battle. Dad was smart, in fact, to this day I believe he may be the smartest person I have ever met. However, I knew, and others knew this battle he was fighting, living and breathing was one he would never win.

Again, in North Carolina, Dad refused to sign anything, refused fingerprints and as a result was put in an old jail, an old cell block in Wake County Jail. I recall something being stolen from Dad, and he talked about going to confront the "gamblers" in the middle of the pod, at which time he was taken by guards to an isolation cell where he spent several weeks. *Oh, my heart. How do I sleep at night?*

There was a newspaper clipping, somehow I was able to get my hands on from *The Raleigh Newspaper*. In this article, Dad was quoted as saying, "The *Montana Freemen* have been called anti-government. Nothing could be further from the truth. The

Montana Freemen may be some of the most pro-government people in America, but we are anti-corruption and we do know the difference." In a nutshell, that was Dad's belief. That's what he stood for. When I asked myself time and time again over the years, what happened to my dad, that was the answer. He truly lived and breathed this. This was his passion and he believed it to his core.

Dad would call and speak of sleeping on his mattress, on the floor in the general population of the Wake County Jail. In February of 1997, Dad had a trial. He shared in his letters of this trial. There were plenty of newspaper articles and one with a large picture of Dad, in handcuffs and shackles, I believe being escorted into court. Dad was not easy to have in a courtroom. He knew law and would often share specific US Codes, word for word. This hearing didn't go well, and Dad was eventually removed from the courtroom. This resulted in him being taken to another county, and eventually flown to Michigan and held in a cell for a couple of days before returning to Montana.

In August of 1997, Dad was returned to North Carolina. Wilmington, where he noted again he was sleeping on the floor for days and was saddened to share there were people chained to walls in a long hallway due to overcrowding. Here he was sentenced to 360 months, or thirty years, despite the Federal Sentencing Guidelines being seventy-five months for his charges. His charges were Larceny/Theft, Interstate Transportation, Conspiracy & Criminal Forfeiture. How can this happen, the question remained with me for the next twenty-four years. He was then shuffled around for a week—Virginia, then back to Oklahoma and finally he was back in Billings, Montana.

Dad wrote of starvation and torture while back in Montana. He noted in a letter that his common-law wife, my stepmother, was cooperating and in fact hired an attorney to represent her. This made me furious. She was always directing Dad, encouraging him not to cooperate and here she was pleading guilty to transporting stolen property from North Carolina to Montana. Dad always said he had receipts proving every single thing was paid in full, and nothing stolen. It was hard to keep up, hard to follow.

My step-mother was sentenced to three years. Three years. Remember this. Remember she was friends with those in Montana. She encouraged and directed Dad to Montana. All of this was so very hard to soak up, to understand and to live with. The two were not allowed to speak after she served her time. I believe she lied to Dad on several occasions, even told him she had attempted to visit him through a letter from a mutual acquaintance. He believed it, but it was just not true. She had moved on. He believed she was threatened, and this was the reason he never spoke to her again. His last communication with her was in November of 2003 via phone call, the one call she answered after he tried and tried for years.

Spring of 1998, Dad was still in Montana. He had been moved between Boulder and Billings a few different times. He was in isolation in Billings and placed with another one of the Freemen, I believe one of the men who owned the ranch where the stand-off took place. He believed the cell was "bugged" as he somehow had seen cassette tapes in an adjacent utility closet. During this time, he again was sleeping on a concrete floor on a 1 ½ inch plastic covered foam mattress. I received several calls during this time. Being a young mom, working and going to school, I would always do my best to answer his calls. Each call hurt. Each time I would answer the phone I was afraid of what I would hear, although, there was never a call, no matter what was happening, that Dad didn't do the two things he would do for the next twenty-four plus years. He would always pray with me and tell me everything was ok because the Lord was in control, that he was ok.

Dad's version of this time frame was horrific. He often talked about going into jail on June 14, 1996, weighing 205 pounds, and about a year later weighing 155. He had stories of being dragged across the floor into a tv room to watch court on tv, since he was refusing to cooperate. He talked of going on a water strike and having to be taken to the emergency room for IV fluids. All the while, Dad never wavered from his belief in the Lord being in control.

In April of 1998, after a short battle with pancreatic cancer, my grandmother, my beautiful heartbroken grandmother passed away. Dad was able to have a phone call with her prior to her passing. This was hard for him, although he made sure to share, he knew where she was going. He wrote about her for months after that, sharing childhood memories and her love for cooking.

In July of 1998, Dad was taken to Seattle Federal Holding Center. He was only there a short time, and once again returned to Billings for sentencing. Dad was given 11.5 years for the following charges: Bank Fraud, Fugitive in Possession of a Firearm, Threats Against Federal Officials & Conspiracy. 41.5 years total. Dad was forty-six at the time of arrest. I was crushed. He would be near ninety years old, if he could make it that long.

I would vow to walk through this time with him no matter the amount of time. He was my dad, and I knew him, I knew him best.

1000 GIFTS FROM A 7 X 10

CHAPTER 5

In Prison on the Outside

Many letters from Dad, weekly. The letters always had a unique border, sometimes in color, sometimes in pen, along with a handpicked cutout picture from a magazine. These pictures would be taped along the side of the letter or in the corner, always a purpose behind the picture, things Dad loved. An example would be a little picture of a baby elephant. Along the side of the picture Dad wrote: *This youngster follows his mother through thick and thin — learns to be strong for when he/she shall lead. It is the trials in life that culture us for victory celebrations in Yavah, Messiah, Jesus the Christ. You shall be made strong in those adverse conditions you overcome today. Keep following Him who shows us the way! It is the heat, the tension that perfects the steel and makes it sturdy for holding up under conditions for which it is made. Keep the faith moving forward for the victory. — September 2016 Russell D. Landers*

The brilliancy of my dad's writing demonstrated his love, the reminders of the power of prayer, and sometimes memories of better times. He shared his heart, a lot of his thoughts on what was happening to him, and a lot of his legal jargon. I would write back, not nearly as often, and not nearly as much as I wish I had.

I would send pictures, although there were times he never got them.

Dad had been in El Reno for a short time when I decided I really needed a visit. I needed to see him. It had been so long—nearly three years with only random phone calls and the exchange of letters. I always found it difficult to write, I wanted things back to how they had been before dad joined this group. Family time, church, visiting grandparents, fishing, and our Disney trips. This all happened so fast, and time was going quickly, well at least for me it was, and doing the exact opposite for dad.

Mom, my little brother Mike, and Alex all took the twelve hour trip to El Reno. I knew this would be hard, I knew my heart would ache, but I just needed to see my daddy. We arrived in El Reno the night before the visit. The excitement my body felt from my head to my toes wouldn't let me sleep that night. Alex, Mike, and Mom were all sound asleep when I got out of bed and walked around the perimeter of the hotel, alone, praying for our visit. "Lord, let him be okay, Prepare me for the heartache ahead of time Lord. Jesus give me strength, give Dad strength." What I found is you cannot prepare enough for seeing the man you love so dearly, with every fiber of your soul, in a jumpsuit, in prison.

The next morning, Mom drove us over to the prison. I see it as vividly as if I saw it this morning. The white truck driving the perimeter of the tall, chain link fence. The guard towers with men armed with rifles. The rows of razor wire the entire perimeter of the fence. I became ill. Tears fell. My heart felt like it was drowning with every breath I took. Mom chose not to go in. I didn't blame her. Alex, Mike, and I went through a rigorous check-in process. Pat search, scanner and even a drug test, which entailed an officer wiping a circular piece of paper across my hands and placing the paper in a machine. The trauma I relived in the moments of being searched almost turned me away. I stayed strong; he was so close.

We walked through an outside area and into a visiting unit. The unit was about the size of two and a half elementary classrooms. There were chairs with small coffee-like tables in the middle. There were several vending machines and even a mural on the wall. An officer directed us where to sit, and I sat, nervous, afraid, and alert to my surroundings. The events in New York changed me, I became hypervigilant to everything around me.

Men came in, one at a time, wearing a light brown button up shirt, light brown pants with an orange label over the upper right chest area.

There he was. THERE HE WAS! The last time I looked dad in the eye, the last time my daddy hugged me was nearly four years ago, as we stood in the Raleigh-Durham airport hotel lobby. We ran toward one another. The guard asked me loudly to "stay in my table area." Oh Daddy, tears, my heart beating faster than ever, and I was hugging him. The course life had taken us had brought us to this very moment, hugging in a Federal Correctional Institution visiting room. "Dad, meet your grandson, Alex." Dad hugged Mike, oh did he hug Mike. Mike was now a 16-year-old young man, and when dad left, he was a tender, 11-year-old. The tears fell and Dad turned to Alex, "Hello son." Alex, nearly 3 years old, looked up at his new grandpa and reached out to him. Dad picked him up and smiled, that smile could be felt across the room. He held him, hugging him and rubbing the back of his head. Tears. There were tears from all of us, well, maybe not Alex, but this moment, this treasured moment brings joy to my heart as I write. I was back with Dad, he was alive, he looked good, and he was now sitting next to me.

We spent the entire visit, from 8:00 a.m. to 3:00 p.m., telling stories, reading the ingredients on the back of our pop cans and snacks and listening to Dad tell us just exactly what these ingredients were. He asked more than once that day, "Do you want THAT in your body?" In this new life, Dad found a lot of time to do research, although he knew this prior to his incarceration, the ingredients being put in foods and pop were just not good for you. He shared with us that our bodies need God's food and told us of how difficult this was in his current circumstance. There were a few times during this visit, I would catch him staring, either at myself, Mike or Alex, a stare that made me feel like he was taking in every second, maybe using his brain like a video recorder, to capture the moments.

About ten minutes before 3:00 p.m., the lights flickered. An officer said to wrap up visits and "inmates to the back of the room, visitors to the front." Dad prayed with us, and I joined in with him. We specifically prayed this would end soon, we prayed that the forty plus years would be overturned, somehow, some way. I hugged Dad, I didn't want to let go. Mike and Alex followed suit and I reached and grabbed him one more time. More tears. We stood in a single file line, with our backs to the wall, and the inmates did the same. It was near torture to stare across the room at Dad, tears in his eyes, so painful he turned around and faced the wall. Just too painful. I held Alex and walked behind Mike as we were escorted out of the visiting room, down a sidewalk back into the room we checked in at, through the gates, the barbed wire, the chain link fences to the parking lot, to find Mom, who was waiting. Lesson learned on this day—nothing produces intimacy like shared suffering. Our relationship only grew stronger due to our suffering—this I knew for sure.

We went straight back to the hotel, and there my mom was

video recording us with her handheld camera. I watched it years later and was taken back by my demeanor. I was quiet, my face empty—it resembled my heart. Again, I was broken, lost, and hurt. *How do I leave him? Should I move here so I could go see him every day?* Oh, the thoughts of a daughter with an incarcerated father. *This wasn't fair, how will I do this for forty years? Something has to be done, there has to be a way to overturn that sentence which was so far out of the guidelines. Twenty-five years more than the guidelines.* Again, this ran through my head countless times throughout Dad's incarceration.

Letters continued. Dad never failed to send me stories of the Bible, stories of what was going on in his day-to-day life, the books he read, and the questions he had for me about life, and our family.

My older brother, Ryan, had graduated from the University of Iowa in the summer of 1999 and stayed in Iowa City and got into the graduate program. He loved classes, although he never admitted to being a *Hawkeye*. He had a passion and a love for the *Panthers* of the University of Northern Iowa, which was down the road from Mom's. Ryan had written Dad one letter, which was well written, as Ryan was one of the smartest people I knew. This letter began with, "Dad, I hope this letter finds you well." He shared his role in Mike's life since Dad's departure when Mike was only ten, he shared of his love for skiing, learning politics and how to build a computer. The letter never shared his anger for Dad, only that he was successful and would make sure Mike succeeded. Dad kept this letter; it meant the world to him.

In January of 2000, Ryan left Iowa City and headed to Chicago for a ski trip with his former roommate from college and best friend. A Friday afternoon, skis in the SUV, Ryan and his best bud took off to Wisconsin. While on I-95, a couple of vans, *playing cat*

& mouse ran my brother off the road, only to hit a guardrail and end up in a ravine. My brother was killed instantly.

In the fog of this day after learning the news that my older brother, the smart, witty, protector of me and my little brother, was dead, people coming to the house and trying to keep my mother breathing, I was tasked with calling the prison, to notify Dad that his oldest son had been killed in a horrific car accident. I called the prison and spoke with a staff member, who needed all of my brother's information so she could "verify the death." I gave her everything she needed, his name, Ryan Landers, his age, 25, where the accident happened—Portage, Wisconsin. She told me to make sure my phone line was not busy at 7:00 p.m. so Dad could call. I did. I held the old cordless phone in my hand, while barely coherent. At precisely 7:00 p.m., Dad was on the line and could hardly speak. "Amy, what happened?" I shared what I knew of the accident, and Dad could not talk. We sat in silence for a moment. "Where is your Mom, Amy? Is she ok?" I told Dad she was not okay and had to be taken to the emergency room. Crushed, physically ill and lost, Dad in his tears began to pray. This prayer was different, he was hurting and reminded me, to remind everyone in my home that evening, "Jesus is near to the brokenhearted sweet pea, Jesus is with you." I took that opportunity to remind him of the same." Daddy, Jesus is near to you at this moment, since I can't be, Jesus is." He knew this. He felt this and he asked that I take care of my mom and Mike. He shared with me that the Chaplain was with him, and he would be with Jesus, closely in prayer for everyone on that evening. His faith, so strong, he knew Jesus would be with him and this gave me some comfort.

Dad was not allowed a furlough to Ryan's funeral. He knew the date and time and spent this time in worship. He shared with me the intense presence of the Holy Spirit he had throughout the time of the funeral. As hard as this must have been, he never wavered from his faith and understanding of where Ryan was. He had sent a letter for Ryan and asked that I put it in the casket with him, which I did. I never read the letter, that was between Dad and Ryan. In phone calls over the next few months, there were many tears, many questions regarding specifics of the accident and I always kept Dad informed of all events.

A few months after Ryan's death, while visiting my grandfather, he asked me if I would take him to see Dad. My grandfather, a tall, gentle man, had moved into an assisted living facility. No longer on his farm, he was sad, and he was hurting after the loss of his wife and grandson. He said he would pay his way, but just needed to see his son one last time. He insisted. I could not say no, and we planned a trip to Oklahoma. The twelve-hour ride was difficult for Grandpa, he was tall, 6'4 I believe, so long car rides had always been difficult. We drove straight through, and I was able to spend quality time with him. Long hours, lots of stories shared, and for the first time, Grandpa cried. He shared how badly Dad's incarceration hurt him, he shared his disbelief in the length of time dad was sentenced and said numerous times, "It's just not right." I agreed with him, and we continued our drive. Mom and Alex were along, and we enjoyed eating out and just being together. We arrived and got checked into our hotel. I recall lying in bed that night thinking to myself how difficult this visit would be for Grandpa, he was sick, fighting cancer and knew this was "goodbye."

This was one of the harder moments in all of that had happened over the last five years, Dad leaving our family and going to fight a losing battle, living with him, and going to Rikers, leaving him in the airport that day, the death of my grandmother, the death of my brother, and now participating in a visit, where a daddy had to say goodbye to his son.

The same gates, the same barbed wire, the same check-in desk and walk to the visiting room. There we sat as we waited for Dad. Grandpa, Alex and I, watching intently at the door where the inmates came out. I showed Grandpa and told him to "watch there, Grandpa!" Dad came out and we stood up, arms open as Dad quickly walked toward us. We hugged, we hugged all together, more tears, and we spent the day with Dad. I'm not sure about them, but I was dreading the advancement of the clock. *How could we do this? How will they say goodbye? How do I witness this?*

Throughout the visit, we shared memories, memories of Ryan, of Grandma, of events on Grandpa's farm, Grandma's home cooked meals, the animals, the tractors...the emptiness Grandpa was feeling after leaving his farm and going into the assisted living home. There was laughter, tears, and silence. More than once I saw Grandpa just staring intently at Dad, and Dad staring back. There was hand holding and pats on the knee. Alex was entertaining, easily making his grandpa and great-grandpa laugh out loud without even trying. A day for which I am forever grateful, and know they were too. Time was ticking.

About ten minutes to three, the lights flickered. Dad and I knew what this meant, Grandpa did not. Dad, as always, asked to pray with us, and we all bowed heads and held hands. Tears began to flow and flowed harder when I heard my dad's trembling voice and my grandpa's sniffles. My mind spoke loudly to the Lord, "Lord TOUCH, TOUCH Lord...TOUCH, please Papa, TOUCH." Dad spoke firmly and prayed intently, asking Jesus for grace, and peace that surpassed all understanding, with the ALL very boldly. Grandpa would softly say, "Amen" in agreement. Dad did an amazing job that day. He fought off his sadness, his

hurt, his frustrations, his anger for the lengthy sentence and his prayer touched even those who sat near us. Dad had always been a man of faith. He wandered for a while, but he knew his purpose and knew his Father, and if anyone had faith the size of a mustard seed, it was Dad.

The lights shut off. This was our clue to head to the front of the visiting room, in a single file line along the door, and Dad's clue to head to the back of the visiting room, in a single file line. We hugged, as we did when we entered, a group hug, and then Alex hugged Grandpa. There were tears and I hugged him oh so tightly. I could discern, through his tight hug, he didn't want to let me go, not just because it was me, but because then he would be hugging his dad for the last time. Dad let me go, turned to his dad, who was standing to the right of me, and they both began to cry, a cry hard to put into words. All the emotions came out of those cries for both of them—anger, sadness, grief, yes grief in what they knew would be their last visit. They hugged until the lights once again flashed to immediately head to the front or back of the room. There was swaying in this hug, a grip so tight, so strong, you could not have pried them apart. I watched and put my hands on both of their backs. Tears, so many tears. "Jesus touch, touch Jesus." Of course, my usual routine—just one more hug and we headed to the front of the room, Dad went to the back of the room as instructed. Again, more intimacy in our shared suffering.

Dad knew there was a purpose to his suffering, this was promised by Jesus. He knew he was not alone in his suffering. He knew Jesus also suffered while He was on earth — significantly, all to display the great glory and love of God. (Isaiah 53.3) Dad knew Jesus was a miracle worker, and as he would always say, "God is preparing us for the glory beyond our hurt and our heartbreak. Hallelujah!" Dad would graciously, make it through another very rough moment... and so would Grandpa, who also knew the truth.

We all stood in line to leave, us out the front door and Dad out the back to return to his life as an inmate. Grandpa stared and didn't stop; Dad did the same. As our line walked toward the door, Grandpa stood still, not knowing the line was moving, until I touched his back and said, "time to go, Grandpa." He began to walk, and tears continued to fall as he raised both hands to wave at Dad. This entire time, I was singing worship music, softly, just enough so Grandpa could hear. Dad waived back and as we got to the door, Grandpa looked ahead to step out, and stopped dead in his tracks, turned and blew Dad a kiss and slowly, turned again to walk forward and away from his son for the last time. One last look, I glanced back at Dad, who slightly turned to see is father walk away for the very last time. Oh, the suffering.

This may have been the first time in my life, while walking from the visiting room to the reception building, that I knew why my dad taught me about the Lord, and why my grandfather taught him about the Lord. It was so that I may have comfort in my sadness, and as sad, heartbroken and restless as I was in this moment, the Lord reminded me of my dad's steadfast faith, his unyielding love for Jesus, and for a moment, I was ok, I comforted Grandpa and reminded him of the promises of Jesus. We held hands and walked to Mom in the parking lot.

It was a long drive home; we stopped a couple of times to eat supper or fill up with gas. The car ride was quiet, with little conversation as our hearts sat at our feet. There was a conversation about the length of Dad's sentence, and Grandpa asked more than once, "Is there something I am missing, why did they give him so much time, it's just not right."

I could only share with Grandpa what I knew, and that was he was over sentenced out of North Carolina and given time in Montana, that was to run consecutively. That was it—that was all I had. Once we got back to Grandpa's place, he thanked me. He thanked me several times, he thanked my mom and with a defeated look on his face said, "I got to say goodbye to my son. I am thankful to you for that." I was thankful that Grandpa had the courage to see Dad. This was a moment Dad would talk about for years.

• • •

I was blessed to have my second son, June 10, 2003, Benjamin (Ben). He was perfect—jet-black hair and chunky, all for his mamma to love on. I took him to see Dad, June 24, 2003. Ben, brand new and perfect. Mom, Alex, Ben, and I took another road trip. Mom and I decided for me to take Ben in to meet Dad in the morning, and she would come in and take him for the afternoon so I could spend more time with Dad. We approved this at the check-in, and Alex, Ben, and I again, went through reception, through the barbed wire, the fences and across the sidewalk into the visiting room. We waited and there was Dad, coming through the door. We hugged through more tears, and he took Ben out of my arms. I don't think he ever intended to put Ben down. He held him the entire morning, often just staring at him. Alex would do his usual, and entertain, while Grandpa would laugh, and touch him on his cheek.

About noon, Mom was walking through the doors. Another difficult moment for all of us. Dad and Mom had not seen each other since that day at the Department of Human Services when the elevator door opened. Mom came and sat down, and in her nervousness held a conversation with Dad. There were tears from Dad, not Mom. She was poised and eager to share where she was in her life, after heartbreak, embarrassment, and the hard work to take care of the family Dad left behind.

This was hard for me at times. I didn't want Dad to be hurt any more than he already was, however, I knew Mom had a right to feel the way she did, she was hurt, and hurt badly.

About half an hour went by and Mom was ready to take Ben. We quickly grabbed a picture, Dad of course holding Ben, with a big smile on his face.

Mom and I packed up Ben's things and she reached to Dad for Ben. He held onto him as long as he could before handing him over. More tears, and Dad kissed Ben on the forehead. Mom turned and told Dad to "take care, Russ" and off they went. Alex and I did our best to make the most out of the remainder of the

visit. Every minute we were allowed to be together meant so much to each of us. The lights flickered, and we followed our familiar routine, praying together and going to our opposite ends of the room. Tears, a wave, and out we went. Yet again, there was Mom waiting.

One evening on a phone call, Dad shared, "Well Amy, I guess I'm back in the news again." I had no idea what this meant. We continued our conversation, and after that call I called Mom and told her Dad said he was back in the news. We both turned on one of the national news stations and watched. Sure enough, after watching for about half an hour there was coverage of *Inmates Accused In Copyright Scheme to Win Freedom.* According to this coverage, Dad and a couple others were facing a host of additional charges connected to an ill-fated scheme in which they attempted to copyright their names. Apparently Dad and the others conspired to force prison officials to release them by making exorbitant financial demands for violations of their common-law copyright on their names. At one point, Dad even had a meeting with the warden and offered to negotiate the return of his property if he was freed. Again, my heart beat a little faster, the torture of the unknowns, and fear for my father, despite his strange behaviors.

That evening I walked to my mailbox. There was a large package from Dad, which was not unusual. He would send drawings, articles, and other literature he wanted to share. As I got back into my apartment, I threw the mail on the couch and made supper. After eating, I sat down and opened the package, only to find a separate envelope inside the larger envelope. Something was strange. There were three envelopes containing a lot of paperwork. Inside the last envelope was a letter in someone else's handwriting. As I went through the papers, my jaw dropped to the floor. Is this the deed to the warden's house? My first thought was to call Mom.

I called and in disbelief told her, "Mom, I think I am holding the deed to the warden's home." She asked me to describe to her what I was holding, so I did in great detail. She said, "Amy call the local FBI office immediately!" As hard as that call was to make, I called, as I wanted nothing to do with this. I reported to the agent on the phone, who I was, who my dad was, and what I was holding in my hand. Within fifteen minutes there were two agents at my door, and I handed over the mail.

I cried a lot that night. The last thing I wanted was for Dad to get in more trouble or be hurt physically more than he had already been.

Dad was put in the hole for the next twenty-two months. There were hardly any phone calls, maybe one a month if that. There were letters. Dad continued to write, and I would do my best to return a letter. I wrote a letter to the warden, copied a couple of senators, and asked how someone could be in solitary this long. There was somewhat of a small investigation into the matter and next thing I knew, Dad was being transferred to USP McCreary in Pine Knot, Kentucky.

I visited Dad once while in McCreary. After several calls to the institution, I was given direction on the visiting policy. I drove the nine hours to McCreary alone and had a visit with Dad. He wore his brown shirt and pants, always tucked his shirt in so properly. We had four hours and were able to laugh, cry and enjoy the normal prayers and hugs. To touch him, to hold his hand, to remind him of how much he was loved, was such a blessing. Had I known this would be the last time I touched my dad for the next eleven years, I may have gone back for more than just one hug. I may have held his hand a little longer.

Dad's stay in USP McCreary was short. He was flown back to Oklahoma to face the new charges. In October of 2007, he was taken in chains to the Federal Courthouse in Oklahoma, where he spent the entire day in a holding cell. He again refused an attorney due to his beliefs, and at the end of the day was taken into the courtroom for a hearing. After no resolution, Dad was taken to the Oklahoma County Jail. Here he described filth, overcrowding and outrageous conditions.

Days later he was taken back to the courthouse and described the result of his refusal to enter the courtroom without the removal of the "US Flag" and putting the "USA Flag (without the gold fringe around it)." He was tased in the back with no warning with a 50,000-volt taser and returned to the Oklahoma County Jail, where he was placed in isolation.

Dad shared he could not even write his name for over 24-hours, using the *flex pen* and one sheet of paper he was given in isolation. He talked often about the lasting effects of the taser situation, and what bothered him most was that it was so unexpected. It was inflicted while he was simply talking and attempting to represent himself. He remained in isolation from mid-March to the last week in May.

No letters during this time were allowed. I learned quickly throughout these events, that I needed to maintain contact with someone at the institution where he was confined. I wanted to make certain that they knew he did, in fact, have someone that cared and loved him very much.

In Oklahoma he was sentenced to an additional 180 months, another 15 years to be run consecutively to his other sentence. We were now looking at fifty-five years. No victim, no violence and so completely out of range of the sentencing guidelines. The frustration I felt, let alone what he felt. It almost encouraged his beliefs to another level.

Soon Dad was returned to McCreary and taken directly to the hole. (May 28, 2008) No phone, no one to talk to, no mail. Dad stayed here until July 23, 2008, when he was put in a van along with his property and taken to Terre-Haute, Indiana to the Communication Management Unit, otherwise known as, CMU, The Counter Terrorism Unit, or as Dad would call it, "hell on earth." This would be the worst, most horrific experience of his life, and to walk alongside him, in all the craziness of my life, one of the most difficult and horrific experiences of my life. Hell on earth.

CHAPTER 6

Unknown Caller

The CMU, Communication Management Unit, is located within the perimeters of Terre Haute Federal Prison, an old, run-down building that sat off to the side of the other units. From my own research, I learned this was the old death row building. Little did I know at that time, I would step foot into this *hell* for my visits.

Dad believed the building had been condemned years before. He shared that the roof leaked badly and wasn't repaired until November of 2008. He noted that rain was still "an indoor event." He wrote of using Styrofoam cups as stands to keep his locker above water. Some incarcerated individuals would be forced to sleep on the top bunk because water would run down the walls to the lower bunks. He described, yellow and black mold being everywhere, until gradually over time, the molds were "painted over." He further described this unit looking like an abandoned building in the movies.

I learned though my research that this unit was designed in 2003 to hold terrorists, such as those involved in events within the United States, such as September 11 and the World Trade Center tragedies. Dad described how he felt like he may have been the only Christian for some time, because everyone else was of the Muslim religion. This made me more and more fearful for his safety. The more I read, the more I feared.

One article I read, stated the Federal Bureau of Prisons (BOP) secretly created the CMU units, and were designed to isolate and segregate certain prisoners in the federal prison system from the rest of the BOP populations. There are currently two CMUs, one in Terre Haute, Indiana and one in Marion, Illinois. There are sixty to seventy inmates housed and approximately 60% of the CMU population today is Muslim.

Those detained in the CMUs are completely banned from any physical contact with family or friends. I would learn this firsthand. All other communication was extremely limited, including any interactions with non-CMU inmates, and of course, phone calls with family or friends.

Dad, and others in the CMU were never given a meaningful explanation for transfer to this unit, nor for the extraordinary restrictions to which he was subjected to. The CMU's visitation policy is even more restrictive than that of the SuperMax prisons, where prisoners have over four times more time allotted for visits. Even worse, I learned that there was no appeal process to get him transferred back to the general population.

As far as I knew, Dad always had a clear disciplinary history. With the exception of the new charges he received in Oklahoma, Dad was never a "problem". He was respectful, kind, and was a man who believed in his cause, which of course could always come across as dominating. Nevertheless, these were truly his beliefs. How would he end up in this place?

Looking further into the CMU units, I read how they were designed to hold *dangerous terrorists and other high-risk inmates, which required heightened monitoring of their external and internal communications.* This would be the reason he was so limited on whom he could write and receive correspondence from. Dad's political views were unpopular to many, but how in the world did he end up here? A couple of times, he called the unit, "little Guantanamo."

An article written in 2010, addressed the fact that the first fifty-five prisoners designated to the CMU, forty-five were sent there because of their connection to terrorism, but the other ten were designated due to involvement in prohibited activities related to communication. I believe Dad's incident in Oklahoma was *the driver of the bus that led him to hell.*

Another article noted CMUs also housed *those with unpopular political views.* It is believed many of these people, which included Dad, were brought in as a calculated means to integrate the units after there was a lawsuit stating there was *targeting of the Muslim population within the Federal system.* These inmates were brought in as balancers.

As I continued to research and learn more and more, I had to question why my Dad was placed in this isolation unit when so many inmates within the federal system were more dangerous than Russ Landers and fit the broad guidelines in determining who would be placed in the CMU. Why my Dad?

Some of the guidelines include, no physical contact, no embrace, nothing. This would contradict the BOP's mission statement:

> **It is the mission of the Federal Bureau of Prisons to protect society by confining offenders in the controlled environments of prisons and community-based facilities that are safe, humane, cost-efficient, and appropriately secure, and to provide work and other self-improvement opportunities to assist offenders in in becoming law abiding citizens.**

Phone calls would be scheduled a week in advance. Only two, ten-minute calls per week, and if operations or anything prevented a call, it was lost, no makeup calls.

Dad described plumbing issues, no recreation yard, only a "cage." He noted, "In this 12th year, I was only on grass, or dirt for less than two months."

There was a federal lawsuit challenging the policies and conditions at the two CMUs, as well as the circumstances under which they were established. It involved *due process standards* which would state that procedures used by the BOP to place & retain people in a CMU must adhere to those standards. I believe the lawsuit is still being heard.

I faithfully answered the weekly, scheduled calls, despite whatever may have been going on in my life. I always saw this as a duty of a daughter—to walk alongside dad through all of this. It was an honor as I reflect. The phone calls, from a *No caller ID* always began with the same recording, "This call is from a Federal Prison, to accept the call dial 5 now, to decline the call please hang up." I would anxiously press "5" and there he would be on the other end. Despite any circumstances, Dad was smiling through the phone, I could always feel that.

"There she is, you're sure looking beautiful today!" Phone calls were our lifeline, he would share stories of his war room and I would share mine, he would laugh and remind me, "I get to LIVE in my war room, twenty-two hours a day!" His perception of his condition could only have been from the Lord. Dad would faithfully ask about family, friends and of course, Penny, my Yorkie, who he longed to take for a walk someday. We would laugh, pray together, and attempt to fit a week's worth of our lives in this ten-minute call.

UNKNOWN CALLER

Dad lived in this 7x10 cell. He would walk back and forth and know how many *laps* it took to walk the square mile by Mom's house that he built years ago. In his mind he would go there while he paced, back and forth, back and forth. He wrote of smelling the Iowa fields while he walked, of the sun beaming down on him, which was the reason it was unbearably hot in his cell, at least in his mind.

My daughter was born in April of 2009. There were many calls with Dad, where I would tell him all about her—her beauty, her unmatched personality that would light up a room. I sent many pictures of her and her older brothers. I felt it was time to make a visit to Terre Haute, with my children, so Dad could finally meet Ava and see how much the other two had grown.

November of 2009, I made a call to the institution and scheduled a visit. I had a lot of questions, which were often met with no answers. We drove the five and a half hours and checked into our hotel. The anticipation for this visit was difficult. With all of my recent research into this prison, this specific unit, I found myself afraid. My thoughts wandered and I wondered if I would actually be able to live with what I was about to witness. It had been two years since we had a visit, since I touched him, hugged him, and felt the protection a daughter feels from those hugs. I knew I would not be able to touch him, but I was thankful to be able to see him.

We arrived at the institution, and as in previous visits at the other two institutions, I pulled up to the call box where a guard in the tower asked, "Do you have any weapons or explosives on you or in your vehicle."

"No, I do not." I was directed to pull forward and park in a specific area. As I pulled in, I took note of the prisons, two of them, one to my left looked new and I learned this was maximum security, no windows, just tall walls of concrete. To the right, what looked to be a very old institution, all of the buildings made of brick, the barbed wires, the rows of electric fencing. I parked and looked around, with an emptiness, a hurt inside of my soul. *How could my daddy be here?* Little did I know, this feeling would only get worse as I experienced this visit.

I got all of my children out of the car, my oldest Alex was around thirteen, Ben was now six, and Ava, close to nine months. We walked into the door I was directed to, and inside was a Correctional Officer sitting behind a desk. I found it odd that I was the only visitor in such a large institution. I would later find out, CMU visits are held at different times then regular visits for the rest of the prison population. We were directed to empty our pockets and walk through the metal detector. We complied and I could feel the fear from my boys, the questions that were running through their minds. We filled out a visiting form, which included who we all were, and the license plate number on my car. We then were directed to have a seat to wait for Dad's counselor and a guard to escort us to our visit.

We waited, and eventually a man came through the metal barred door. The door was buzzed open, and he asked that we come with him. Together, we stood inside of the metal bars, as the gate behind us closed and the one in front of us opened. I can still hear it close, BANG. It never failed, the thoughts of that first night in Rikers came back and I was now terrified. I became hot and had to talk to Jesus in order to calm myself. Anxiety, sadness, so many emotions were running through me as I unconsciously carried my daughter, behind my boys and the counselor.

I looked up and saw a sign above one of the brick buildings that read *Visitation*, but we continued walking right past it. We followed a sidewalk, to my left razor wire, 10-foot-tall chain linked fencing with more razor wire, and to my right brown brick buildings, one after the other. I could tell these were dorm style units, they were old, that was obvious as well.

Looking ahead, I noted the building with the green metal roof, it stood out of the lineup of buildings. The counselor took the sidewalk leading to the side of this building. *This must be CMU.* A fence covered the door, and a special key was used to allow us inside of this small fence. Then, I took note of the old style, skeleton key that was used to open the door to the unit.

We were inside what seemed to be a storage area, I quickly took note of the tub labeled, "Landers." We were led to a room, the door made of metal, with the center cut out where glass was. The room was small, maybe 6x9. There was a small toy against the wall, a children's toy, used, very used. It contained only one metal stool with a circular place to sit, and a large window with a black phone on the wall. My boys looked around; they were nervous as the guard shut the door behind us.

Outside of our door, an old wooden desk with an old rotary phone sat in the corner. The boys found a spot on the floor, while I held Ava sitting on the circular metal stool. The sadness of what was transpiring, the anxiety, I felt the weight of the world as I waited to see my dad.

Shortly, on the other side of the glass, my dad was brought in. He was smiling, smiling with tears. He was handcuffed and also had these attached to a belly chain. The guard released one of Dad's hands as he sat on his metal chair. The guard told us to wait to pick up the phone, as Quantico had to be on the call.

Dad and I just stared at each other. Looking into the eyes of a man whom I knew, and knew so well, a man who wouldn't hurt a fly, a man who loved Jesus with every ounce of his being. I held Ava up to the window, the boys put their hands to the window, while Dad put his free hand to the window to try and feel a touch. *How could this be happening?* I didn't understand, I don't understand. *Those crazy thoughts of his, the beliefs he had, does he deserve this? Did Dad's crime fit the time he was given?* Not in a million years did I agree with this, and still to this day do not agree with this. The pain of staring at him, tears in his eyes, as the CO said we could now pick up the phone.

"Hi Daddy!" "Hi sweet pea!" Our conversation flowed; it wasn't forced. This wasn't a letter or a phone call that we had been communicating with over the last three years. I could see him, I could feel him, I could cry with him. I gave the boys each an opportunity to sit on the stool and talk with Grandpa. Their conversations flowed, there was no pause, no need for me to keep the conversation going. For both of them, it was natural, and it was natural for Dad too. He knew them, he knew their likes, their dislikes, their dreams, their hopes for the future. He knew because he would ask. He always wanted to know about them. On each phone call, in each letter, he was intentional about learning about the things going on outside of the walls.

The visit was two hours and flew by. We were directed to end the call, and we of course, prayed together and touched the glass like they do in the movies. It was real to us; the immense pressure of sadness consumed us all that day. The reality of what Dad was going through hit me harder than any other day.

No hug, no kiss for any of us. We blew kisses instead, as we were escorted out first. As always, one last look, smile, and hand in the air as I blew the kiss from my palm. We were then escorted back to the reception area, through the metal bars and we walked back to our car. I had to take a moment, a moment to breathe, a moment to pray outside the institution for Dad and others. I needed a moment to take all that I was feeling and let it go.

After getting home from the visit, I processed with the boys, their thoughts. Alex cried; Ben cried. I found it difficult to know what to say that would comfort them. It was hard for them to understand why they could not hug Grandpa. There were many questions, many difficult questions that I just did not have the answers to. I didn't understand myself.

A few years had gone by, the letters were a constant, the borders drawn with perfection, the cut-out magazine pictures, the little cowboy emblem that Dad put on each and every letter, his very own design of a simple smiley face with a cowboy hat. Weekly, letters came, sometimes addressed to me, sometimes to one of my children. He never missed a birthday, ever. Not for me, my children, my brother or his family, my mother, or his siblings. Not one. We always received a card, no matter what it took on his end, we received a card.

He never asked for anything, no money, nothing. He was content living in his war room, minute by minute, hour by hour and day by day. He read a lot. He loved books like *Battlefield of the Mind* by Joyce Meyers. He would always share knowledge such as, *Remember, thoughts become things Amy. Caution, careful what you are thinking about all day long. See? Make this a fine day! Smile! Matthew 8:13* — August 2019

The next visit, I was without the kids. I took a road trip with my best friend, Angie, to a women's conference near Indianapolis. We tried to get Angie on the visiting list, as she had known Dad her entire life. She was denied, we were *too close to the time we wanted to visit*. This was always so frustrating. The small unnecessary obstacles that only created pain for so many. We pulled

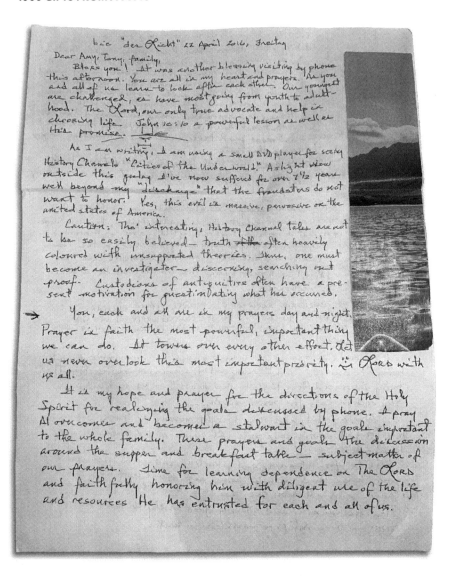

into the institution, back to the call box, and we were asked the same questions. Angie pulled up and dropped me off at the door.

My thought as I walked to the reception door was wanting to run away. *I don't want to do this.* I was reminded of Hebrews 13:3 *Continue to remember those in prison, as if you were there yourself. Remember also those being mistreated, as if you felt their pain in your own bodies*. This gave me strength, all of the strength I needed to walk into this hell on earth to my daddy.

I went through the check-in procedures, filled out my paperwork, showed my ID and waited on the counselor to escort me. I was taken down the same path, and this time held a conversation with the counselor. He shared with me, "Your dad is a neat guy, Amy. He may have a chance to move out of this unit sometime, he isn't a problem whatsoever." This was music to my ears and in that moment, the courage I walked in with, the shield of the Lord, gave me more hope. I thanked him for sharing this and shared how special my dad is, his heart and his love for Jesus. I wanted him to understand, to know my dad, really know the person my dad was.

I was taken through the gated door, through the metal door, back through the entry/storage area into my little room, and locked in. The door shut behind me, and there I sat, as Dad was brought in on the other side. Handcuffed to his waist, one hand released, we waited for the phone to be ready to talk.

The clear was given and we raced to pick up the phone. We shared recent events in our lives, and we smiled. We shared memories and smiled more. We shared thoughts from recent letters, and we smiled. Oh, how I needed this time with Dad.

At one point I was reminded of a recent letter from him where he shared about a Somalian pirate whom he became friends with during his short hours out of his cell. He said the man had been in a movie starring Tom Hanks. Out of plain curiosity I asked him, "How is the Somalian man, Dad?" It was seconds later and the phone at the desk outside of my door rang, and the CO sitting at the desk answered the call. He stood up, unlocked Dad's door and said with a stern voice, "Landers don't talk about the pirate."

Dad responded, "Oh I apologize, I didn't know I couldn't talk about my friend." I immediately jumped in, if only so the person listening would know, I did not intend to get Dad in trouble, and I was very sorry for asking about his friend and student. Dad was teaching him to read and speak English. That was all I knew and the purpose of me asking about him. Dad was always tickled about the progress his friend was making.

The visit was soon coming to an end. Two hours flies when you only see your dad behind glass maybe once a year at this point. We touched our hands to the glass. For some reason, there is comfort in doing this when you are not able to touch your loved one. I had seen it on television before and wondered—it was as close as we could physically be. And so, our hands to the glass, phone resting on our shoulder, I began to pray, Dad would shout, "Amen" in agreement with my prayer. Dad took over and we prayed for traveling graces and for an end to our nightmare as we had now done for almost fifteen years.

I went to the door and did my usual turn around, not for a hug this time but for a hand-to-hand touch through the glass, and off I went.

Getting to the car, Angie waited for me. She was great at taking pictures and she shared with me the beautiful pictures she took, of such an ugly place. She wrote across the pictures, Hebrews 13:3. Wow Lord, this was on her heart too.

Years in CMU continued to go by. Every holiday, every birthday, so many missed. I would try to visit dad at least once a year, I would always hope for more, but as a single mom, he always understood my struggles.

• • •

June 2012: For months Dad would talk about a small rash of blisters that started on his lower right ankle. By July this rash had spread to other areas, his chest, back and upper arms. He was allowed to see a Physician's Assistant (PA) and was diagnosed with a heat rash. He was given Hydrocortisone cream. There was little to no relief. He continued to use the cream and would tell me over phone calls how difficult it was. He estimated the temperature to be over 110 degrees in his cell during the day. On more than one occasion he would pass out from no air circulation. He would talk about getting ice when he was out of his cell and placing the ice bucket behind his small fan to have some temporary cold air. This relief would last less than five minutes as the ice melted. Sleeping was dreadful. He would strip down to his boxers, after soaking them in cold water and lay very still. However, the rash was getting worse.

December 2012, now nearly seven months with this unknown rash, Dad would see the PA yet again. He was told the condition was possibly a bacterial infection, even though his right foot and bottom seemed unaffected. Dad was prescribed a medication, 100mg of Doxycycline for fourteen days, which he shared with me and noted, he took faithfully. The pain, the itching was so unbearable, he cried when we shared a phone call. He described that during the course of the antibiotics, his condition continued to worsen as he was now having bowel issues. On Christmas Eve, he was able to see a nurse who made a couple of calls, resulting in another course of the same antibiotic. He received the second dose on 12/27/2012. Still no positive results, and continuing to get worse, he describes the intensity and how the rash was now covering his entire body except his left foot and bottom. Daily, new breakouts, and no actual diagnosis.

Finally on January 8, 2013, he was again seen by the PA.

(8 months) He ordered that Dad get an appointment with an outside dermatologist or photos be taken and sent to a dermatologist for evaluation, diagnosis, and treatment. Also, that Dad receive three Benadryl shots in three consecutive evenings for itching, and that blood should be drawn for evaluation.

A week went by, none of the above was done.

I made a call to the prison and spoke with Dad's counselor and shared my concern for his health and lack of treatment.

January 15, 2013, a nurse, and a department head went to speak with Dad. They looked over his *array of boils and wounds*. They informed him they would administer more Benadryl shots and the blood work would be done.

At 7:30 p.m. on January 15, 2013, a nurse administered a Benadryl shot. At 3:00 a.m. the next morning, Dad awoke in unbearable pain and could not sleep due to extreme itching and burning. Once let out for his brief, out of cell time, he asked an officer to get someone to see him asap. At 9:00 a.m., the nurse came to see him. They spoke about his worsening condition, his inability to sleep and swelling of his right foot and leg. She arranged for the doctor to come that afternoon. The doctor arrived at Dad's cell at 1:50 p.m. He examined Dad and asked a few questions. He re-ordered the Benadryl shots and ordered *Permethrin Cream* for scabies. That afternoon this photo was taken.

This continued for months. Nothing was working. Finally, a new medication was prescribed, and Dad believed this medication was for Shingles. The boils and rash began to disappear. He believed he had Shingles the entire time, nearly a year before it was resolved completely.

• • •

November 2018, an incident that would send chills up my spine even as I write occurred. For eleven years, he was only permitted out of his cell for a few hours each day. If Dad missed a few calls, I would always reach out and maintain contact with the prison. Again, it was important to me, and important to Dad that someone cared.

The following is a letter I sent to anyone I could think of, Iowa senators, the warden, and Dad's counselor. I felt it was important to add this letter because of the details of the lack of compassion for a daughter, in my fear, my hurt and my soul's cries.

1000 GIFTS FROM A 7 X 10

Written: December 17, 2018:

Dad had three missed calls, on 11/12, 11/14 and 11/19 I began to become concerned. I attempted my first phone call to Terre Haute on Tuesday, 11/20/2018 at 1530 hours and after no answer I attempted twice more at 1533 and 1540 hours. The phone rang & rang and then began to beep. I followed up on Wednesday, 11/21 at 1500 hours and again at 1515 hours — again, no answer.

On Thursday 11/22 an operator answered my call. I asked if I am able to talk with someone regarding my father's safety. I was directed to his counselor. I left a detailed message requesting a call back to help ease my concerns of my father's safety. On 11/26, another attempt to follow up with my message to his counselor, I again received no answer at the prison.

11/26/2018 — 1800 hours: I received a call from my father. It was obvious something was different because despite my father's circumstance he remains steadfast in his faith and assuring me by his joy that all is well. He stated his cell neighbor, a 78-year-old man was stabbed eighteen days ago, and prior to this, approximately ten minutes earlier, his best friend of the last eight years, a 68-year-old man Robert was murdered. At this time, he believes due to religion, but he really was not sure. He was very concerned as these two inmates are his closest friends on the unit.

I asked my father wasn't this strange since this unit is more for high-profile crimes and there hasn't been any violence that I was aware of in his eleven years here. He stated the unit was the Counterterrorism unit and is very dangerous. He stated on more than one occasion he is afraid what will happen when the men are released back to the unit although he had no indication of when this would happen. When asked about the attacker, he stated he had been on the unit for maybe three years, and that he had not had an issue with this man, and neither did Robert or the 78-year-old man. He was in "shock" I guess at this point. I informed my father I would continue to try and contact the prison to gain some understanding of the safety plan to keep him and the other elderly men safe. He stated he would be given another call at noon tomorrow.

11/27/2018 noon: Call from Dad who again sounded nervous and scared. He stated the 78-year-old man was alive and had been stabbed eleven times. He stated it is not safe here and that there is a very violent group of Jihad people, and the attack was believed to be over religion, as these men are Muslim. He stated an investigator told him that morning there are five men on a list who are targets of this Jihad group — and he is on the list. The five men included Robert who was murdered and the 78-year-old man who had been so brutally attacked. He stated at one point he thought they may move him and the other three elderly men out of the unit. He stated they are letting them out one at a time for little periods of time, otherwise they are in their 7x10 cell day and night.

11/28 — Wednesday — called FCI Terre Haute — no answer.

11/30 — Friday — Called FCI Terre Haute — no answer

12/3 — Monday — Called FCI Terre Haute — no answer

- *Afternoon call — answered — was directed to Dad's counselor. Operator stated this was the only authority he had was to transfer the call to Dad's counselor. Left a detailed message.*

12/4 — Tuesday — Called — operator directed me to Dad's

counselor. No answer Left detailed voice mail.

- *Afternoon call — no answer.*

12/5 — Wednesday — Talked to Dad (1800 hours) He was getting a couple hours a day out of his cell. Stated he on a "hit list" from ISIS. Asked if I knew who ISIS was. He stated this is who was responsible for the attack on Robert and the 78-year-old man. He states he is definitely not safe here and had heard they attempted to cut off Roberts head in the attack. He stated he was not sure if this was true, but this is what was being said.

12/7 — Friday @ 1035 hours: called — no answer

- *1036 hours — no answer*
- *1435 hours — no answer*

12/10 — Monday — 1256 hours: Operator answered, informed him I had been trying to reach a counselor for over a week and have had no response. He stated I could write a letter to the warden, however there was not a supervisor I could talk to. I notified him this is a possible safety concern I have for my father who is an inmate, and I was desperate to speak to someone. I was again forwarded to Dad's counselor where I again left a voice mail.

12/11/2018 @ 0803 hours: Operator answered — shared my attempts to reach someone in regard to the safety of my elderly father. Stated "I am just the front entrance guy; I will ring you to his counselor." Again, left a voice mail.

- *1037 hours: Spoke with my pastor , Quovadis Marshall. Having a hard time with this.*
- *1111 hours: Spoke with Governor Ernst' Office. Left a*

detailed description of my concerns with a case investigator. They will look into anything they can help with.

- *1123 hours: Spoke with Senator Grassley's office — they will contact a state staffer and direct me to someone to talk to immediately. Spoke with Valeri — she is emailing a form, to be returned. They will then take it to the Judiciary Committee in DC who will get some answers from Terre Haute. We will have an opportunity to ask questions and have them answered.*

All of the above documented information to say the following: As a citizen of the United States of America I am highly concerned with the treatment in so many ways of my father, Russell Dean Landers. It is my understanding the foundation of the Bureau is to have sound correctional management, maintaining effective security and control in the least means necessary. This is not happening within the system of Terre Haute when staff do not consider the public's pleas for a desperate response to the safety of an inmate who has not only a threat of death, but a group who has proven what they will do both prior to incarceration and while incarcerated. Is it not the responsibility of the prison to provide a safe environment for inmates? How are these inmates housed, if according to violence propensity, this is way off in this unit? How is the dignity of my father, a human being recognized — isn't the prison system and the incarceration itself the punishment? Is there an assessment used to determine the risk of inmates? Is there a policy detailing maintaining inmates safety, due process — and if so is this being followed — who is monitoring?

And my three biggest questions...

1. *Why are elderly Christian men being housed with AL Qaeda/ISIS members who are violent, were violent and*

continue to be a threat?

2. Why has nobody from the prison responded to my messages after weeks of calling?

3. What is the plan moving forward knowing my father is a target of the 11-12 ISIS members on his unit to ensure my father's safety?

I appreciate this situation being brought to the front of peoples' thoughts if even only for a moment. This situation does not go away for me, and surely not for my father. I appreciate those who will help me receive answers and make sure that our system is keeping inmates safe during their incarceration. I also appreciate those who will help take steps in the criminal justice reform of the federal system taking place at this time.

The mission of the BOP is to protect society by confining offenders in the controlled environments of prisons and community-based correctional facilities that are safe, humane, cost efficient, appropriately secure, and provide work and other self-improvement opportunities to assist offenders in becoming law abiding citizens.

I would like to see the staff and inmates following these missions and be monitored effectively to ensure the prison is meeting the minimal standards of their own mission.

Sincerely,
Amy Landers

I documented all of the above to see if there was any help out there. I was helpless, I was desperate for someone to help my dad. He was now sixty-nine years old, had been incarcerated for twenty years, he was fragile. I received a letter from both senators, and there was someone reaching into the institution to see if there was anything they could do. This allowed me to breathe, to

UNKNOWN CALLER

go to work and function and to be a mother to my children, when my heart was broken.

March 19,2019: I received a letter from Senator Earnt's office.

I prayed. I prayed a lot, specifically for Dad's safety, for someone to help. In June of 2019, while driving to work my phone rang. *Unknown Caller*. This was not Dad's scheduled time to call but I answered. "This call is from a Federal Prison…" I immediately began pressing 5 and Dad was on the other end of my line. "DAD!" With tears, and smiles that I felt through the phone, he said he had been taken out of the CMU unit. Eleven years in horrific conditions. He was out and in the general population. His joy could be felt, not just heard.

We did it! Dad began to share, "Amy, I can see the sky! I haven't seen the sky in eleven years." *Dear God, what did I just hear? Eleven years in the CMU, and when he was in the cage outside, there was a covering over it.* I never thought of this. I celebrated with him, while he shared he was able to now walk the track. He shared as if he had just won a large lottery jackpot. "Oh Amy, the sky, the track, I don't have to pace in my cell for hours anymore! I can call you whenever I want, no more scheduled calls!"

Oh, the joy in my heart, he was happy, he was so very happy! When the phone call ended, thirty seconds went by, and my phone rang again. Unknown caller. "This call is from a Federal Prison." "Dad?" "I can call you again and again—thank you Jesus for this privilege. Thank you Jesus for hearing our prayers!"

Dad called five times within that hour and again, several times that evening. His newfound freedom to use the phone had him the happiest he had been in over twenty years; I am sure of it.

The next day, June 10, was Ben's 16th birthday. We jumped

in the car and headed to Terre Haute. I could now TOUCH my dad and there was no time to waste. Ben, Ava and I drove five and a half hours and arrived at our hotel. We spent that evening swimming at the hotel and eating a great supper together. We had a lot to be thankful for in that moment. We would now get to spend time with Dad, in a regular visit. Dad could finally touch Ava and Ben! The last time he touched Ben was when he was only fourteen days old. Ben was excited for the opportunity to give his grandfather a hug, finally. Ava was excited to hold Grandpa's hand and eat snacks. We could hardly sleep.

The next morning, we prepared ourselves, got dressed and drove over to the prison. Stopped at the entrance, the call box asked us the same questions. We were directed to park. We did, and excitedly walked into the reception area. This was new, there were others signing in and going through the security procedures. I felt normal, I felt Dad was normal, I felt joy. I handed the CO sitting behind the desk my ID and told them who I was there to visit, Russell Landers, 05177-046. The CO asked who I had with me, Ben & Ava. He immediately asked, how old is Ben? My heart stopped as I answered, "He's sixteen, he turned sixteen yesterday." Does he have an ID? Ben pulled his billfold out of his back pocket and proudly handed over his new license, which he had just gotten the day before on his sixteenth birthday, his *official* driver's license." The CO sternly said, "He can't visit, he's sixteen." I came back quickly telling the CO that Ben has always been on Dad's visiting list, for the last sixteen years. The CO said that once you turn sixteen, a complete FBI background check would need to be done, and this takes at least two weeks. I told the officer, I would need to talk to someone, someone who could make this right. I explained my Dad, Ben's grandfather, had only held him when he was fourteen days old — that WAS IT. I told him Dad had been in the CMU unit for eleven years and was just released, this was Ben's first opportunity to hug his grandfather. The CO said he would call a supervisor.

Ben was horrified, he was sad, and he was angry, all in one facial expression. A supervisor came to the front desk and shared the policy of a sixteen-year-old visiting. I asked that an exception be made, as we only visit once or twice a year, Ben had never had a visit that wasn't behind glass, please, please make an exception.

He had been 16 for less than 12 hours.

The supervisor said the rule was the rule and walked away.

Ben turned away too, with a tear running down his cheek.

He said, "Mom, you and Ava go in and see Grandpa. You hug him for me, Mom." Ben would then use his new *official license* to drive over to the mall while waiting for our visit to end. Heartbroken, he walked out the door.

More tears fell as I stood in a group with others. We were escorted through the metal bars, and Ava and I, hand in hand walked into the visiting room. I looked down the sidewalk and saw that building with the green roof, and I was more thankful than ever that I did not have to take that walk on this day.

Once inside the visiting room, the CO told us where to sit. There were two long rows of chairs, and chairs behind them in another row. We were directed to sit in the last chairs in the row. I quickly learned the door where inmates were coming out. I waited, knees shaking, eleven years I have waited for this hug and so had Dad. Soon, the door opened and there he was. He stood and looked around, wearing a bright, yellow jumpsuit that all inmates had on. I noticed his collar was tucked in and falling off his shoulder. He looked lost, and so I said, "Dad, Daddy, I'm here, I'm right here Daddy."

He heard my voice, turned and quickly walked to me. A CO came over and told him he needed to go check-in. I went with him, and he told the CO his name. They explained to him all hugs would need to be done here in the front before and after the visit. I turned and hugged Dad tighter than I had ever hugged him before, Ava hugged her Grandpa for the first time in her ten years of life. He was fragile, he was almost afraid to be touched, he was afraid. *What had happened to my dad?* Oh Lord this was so hard, so much to take in. I held his hand and walked him over to our designated seats. He sat down, crossed his legs and his arms and leaned over his lap. His body language told me he had been hurt; however, I knew in my heart he would never tell me.

We had two hours together. We attempted to share stories, but Dad was somewhat non-verbal. He looked around the room, stuck in a stare here and there until I said more. He would look at me and at Ava, and it seemed like nothing else in the world was there. He would go into moments of frozenness. I did my best to make him laugh, to hold his hand and help him to feel safe, if even for a moment.

Despite Dad's new housing area, something was very different. Maybe it was because he had gotten older since our last visit and was now sixty-nine years old. Maybe it was all of the years in prison taking its toll. The last eleven years had been tough—the isolation, the despair he lived with, was it all too much? If I was feeling the brokenness, the injustice of this elderly man doing years, and years in a cell, I could not imagine how outraged Jesus was with my dad's situation, let alone, our entire system as a whole.

We ended the visit, as directed. Dad was told to line up at the door he had entered only two hours before. Ava and I were directed to the front of the room. As always, we ended with prayer.

I specifically asked Jesus for healing over my dad, he was so fragile, so broken, so worn. I held Dad's hand, Ava's hand in between, and we spoke to our Heavenly Father. Dad whimpered, the tears, they were genuine, the emotions were there, just slow moving. Slow movements and slow responses.

Dad went in the door, he didn't look back, he was doing his best to focus on the things around him. I watched as the large metal door closed, and the glimpse of the yellow jumpsuit disappeared.

When I left that day, and got into the car with Ben, who was in the parking lot waiting. I was numb. There were tears, but my body ached, and my heart felt frozen. With worship music playing, we took the long drive home. Ben shared his frustration with their lack of compassion. He was angry. He didn't understand, and once again, neither did I. I had no words to explain how or why he was denied a visit. *Had this been a policy for a long time, and if so, why hasn't it been changed? Why wouldn't this child, yes child, young adult, be given the opportunity to visit with his elderly grandfather.*

I was angry too.

1000 GIFTS FROM A 7 X 10

CHAPTER 7

Returning to the War Room

Over the next month, Dad would share his newfound freedoms, since being out of the CMU unit. He would often share during our non-scheduled, anytime he wanted phone calls, his thankfulness to be out of that unit. Dad's sores had healed, and he seemed to be doing better, despite his circumstances. His faith remained and hope for his liberty never wavered. Phone calls, sometimes three or four a day, would bring him so much joy, it could be felt through the phone. He often shared the time he spent on the track, and the new friends he met along the way. His letters still arrived as they always had, every week, sometimes addressed to me, sometimes one of my children. How I loved when Dad would share the Word, share how proud he was of them, and share things that I had told him about the kids. He always remembered. He was intimately involved in our lives, through phone calls and letters, he truly was able to make it seem as if he was right here the whole time.

In July of 2019, suddenly there were no phone calls, they stopped. One day turned to two, two to three, and my subconscious told me to call the institution. Something had to be wrong. After several calls with no answer, I was referred to Dad's counselor. I was told he was ok, but they couldn't share why he wasn't calling.

Days turned to weeks. With anxiety running through my veins, I called again. There was no information anyone could give me. A month, no calls. I felt helpless, and even called to talk with a supervisor, who also would not give me any information. I was helpless, hopeless and concerned—with no options, nothing. I knew he was showing signs of aging and was firm in his beliefs. *Did he make someone angry?* When your elderly father is incarcerated, the endless thoughts that run through your mind drive you to a dark hole of depression, where your body goes on with daily tasks, but your heart is bare and raw to the realities of what you live with day after day.

During September, the agony continued. Not even a letter. No help from anyone. I received a phone call late one afternoon. *Unknown caller*. After the millionth reminder the call was from a Federal Prison, Dad was on the other end. My voice cracked and tears fell as I heard and felt the same coming from him. He said he had been in *the hole* after being accused of *a claim of possession of a fraudulent financial instrument*. He described this piece of paper as an "illustration like one would see in a business law book and could never be fraudulent. It was a drawn check, handwritten, and I didn't even know it was in my possession." He was broken yet able to cover this well. He shared he had no radio, wore orange clothes and had no food from commissary, which he had become used to over the last month. He said a nice officer wheeled a phone stand down to his cell and allowed him to call me. Oh, my despair—his despair. He reminded me yet again of who was in control. He would do his best to contact me when he was released, and he hoped this would be soon. I missed our daily calls. It had been eleven years of scheduled, short, calls. We found a new life in being able to talk freely; it was so good for our hearts and mental health. Note I said, *ours*.

Another month, *Unknown Caller*, and Dad was on the line. He was hurting, frustrated, angry, and—back in CMU. If only I could have reached through the phone to hug him and tell him how sorry I was. He was horrified, he was angry, he was hurt. He shared they *lost* or wouldn't return his property—some books, approximately $100.00 of commissary, but worst of all, the only letter he had from my brother, Ryan. It was all gone. He was later told someone threw all of his stuff away. The pain this caused his heart, the grueling pain, that he just had to live with. I wrote a letter to the institution about his belongings, receiving no response or help.

The scheduled calls, not being able to see the sky, no track, no freedom to come out of his cell—once again all gone. His *war room* was on the second floor and his safety, again at risk.

COVID-19 began, and this was tough for all institutions I'm sure. For the CMU inmates, this meant staying in your cell twenty-four hours a day, seven days a week, with one hour out every three days to shower, send an email, get your ice bowl to put behind your fan and make your call. A 7x10 cell, with no air circulation, and a small foggy window. Dad would describe it as letting light in but seeing out was impossible. Twenty-four hours a day. After a couple months of this schedule, he would get two hours out a day, but then, back to the twenty-four. The seconds, the minutes, the days, nights, were excruciating.

Dad shared he had fainted, which he said was because of the heat, on more than one occasion. This schedule went on for nearly two years. Dad's days were spent writing letters, reading his Bible, walking the "square block at Mom's" and napping. He never complained about it, he would just say, "this is what it is" and go on with the conversation, hoping to hear of some good news, and praying over me and my kids, my brother's family and of course, Penny. We always found some peace in the fact we were *sleeping underneath the same big sky.*

I was scrolling Facebook one day and found a page entitled: *FAMM: Families Against Mandatory Minimums,* when I noticed an article posted about Compassionate Release. I began to research what all this entailed and found that FAMM was helping families find representation at no cost to assist in getting those out of prison who met the requirements of *Compassionate Release.* I immediately, without hesitation, filled out the application. Within a couple of weeks, I received a call from a representative who wanted to interview me in regard to Dad's case. She asked a lot of questions and felt he would definitely be a good candidate. He met the requirements, although he didn't have a terminal illness (that we knew of), he did have a long history of asthma and bronchial issues, that could be an issue if he were to contract COVID-19. She was empathetic, listened to my cries, and believed she would be able to help me find an attorney to start the *Compassionate Release* process. Oh, the joy I felt hearing these words. This could be the answer to our prayers—freedom and fishing. This could be the beginning of Dad coming home to me and living out the remainder of his years with me, my children, and Penny. After everything we had all been through, especially Dad—the years of solitary, the CMU and the horrific stories of injustices, this could be wrapping up after twenty-two years. Could it be?

I was able to share this phone call with Dad and the news of having someone help us fight for his release. Dad was elated. He was smiling from ear to ear, his newfound hope would bring joy to a soul that had been yearning to be back home with his family for years, a soul that had been cooped up in a cell for years. He deserved this.

Within a week, I received a call from Raleigh, North Carolina. Normally, I would not answer these calls from a different state, a number I didn't recognize, but something told me to answer this call. On the other end of the line, a soft, caring voice asked if I was Amy. She introduced herself as "Kat" and stated she was a federal defense attorney, who had been notified by FAMM of my our case. I began to cry silent tears. Kat asked questions, she listened intently, she empathized with my heart. She heard me. She said she would begin working on Dad's case. As we knew, there were no promises, but she felt he had met the requirements due to his age, his length of time served and his health being in jeopardy because of COVID-19. Kat began reviewing Dad's case prior to our call and said due to the complexity of the different locations and charges, this would take time, but she reassured me, and comforted my heart in more ways than she will ever know. Kat would be in contact with Dad at some point and would be back in contact with me as needed.

I was and am eternally grateful for Kat. Dad was too. He shared when she first O-mailed him. He reminded me to pray for Kat and her team each and every phone call, to which I did and already had been doing.

Over the next several months, Dad would call at his scheduled times, his hopes and desires for me and my children, and himself were always a topic of conversation. He shared how his days all blurred together, as they had for years. He spoke often of the "horrific" food he was given to eat, explaining a piece of cheese on the bologna sandwich was some type of "wax" and he would take it out into the cage when allowed to feed some stray cat that stood outside of the fence. He laughed and in seriousness said, "I could be charged with animal cruelty giving that to the poor cat, it is wax, it has to be." Dad found it very difficult to eat "God's food" with such limitations. There were days he spoke of eating peanuts, a handful of peanuts because the food was not edible. He would speak of the hours he spent reviewing his housing situation, and he had calculated just over nine years total in the hole, solitary. For months he spoke of his property that was taken and never returned. Listening to him describe the incalculable value of Ryan's letter, he never spoke of this without having to stop talking, and just breathe through the tears. He would share about his frustration with being in the CMU—being held with violent terrorists who had murdered before, murdered his best friend. The times he was restricted from the phone over the years, the only contact with me taken, and how this hurt his soul, and he understood how this hurt my soul, my heart. He would speak of Jesus, and of his concern with our system not reflecting the God-given dignity and potential of the people. He would speak of the harsh-disproportionate sentencing, and the time being stacked and run consecutively. Through all of those conversations, his hope, his faith, and the hope of the Gospel shined through. The fact that he had read the Bible all the way through twenty-one times, influenced his conversation, his heart and his perception of life from behind the walls. He knew and he fully believed there was a purpose for prison, and he was there for a reason.

Isaiah 40:31 — But those who have hope in the Lord will renew their strength — they will soar on wings like eagles, they will run and not grow weary, they will walk and not be faint.

Dad lived this verse each and every day.

As seasons progressed, life was ready to throw yet another curve ball. *Would I be ready?* Dad was healthy, my life was going well, and we now had a newfound hope.

CHAPTER 8

Compassionate Release — Is There Compassion?

July of 2020 — Kat was preparing Dad's *Compassionate Release* submission. I learned from her that she was chosen by FAMM to assist in Dad's case because the charges in North Carolina were so far over the sentencing guidelines, we could ask for a reduction to within the guidelines and Dad would be released on time served. She asked that I write a letter to the judge, which would include a little about myself, my age, my occupation, and my children. Share about my childhood, how life was good. Share my concerns for him, his age and his health with the possibility of getting COVID-19, and that I would allow him to live with me if he were released. Share my thoughts on Dad not being a threat, because I knew him best. She asked that I only share "truth" and who my dad was "despite the headlines." She also asked that if anyone else wanted to submit a letter, now would be the time to do so. I reached out and several friends and family agreed.

I immediately wrote to the judge, although I had no idea who this person was, I was eager to share my story, and plead for mercy. I had my letter emailed back to Kat within a week, along with a couple of other letters.

November 12, 2020: Received an email from Kat, she was continuing to work on Dad's motion and was setting up a call with him. He would be ecstatic!

Kat and Dad would communicate via scheduled phone calls and O-Mail. During our calls he was always excited to share with me the things they discussed, and his happiness and joy he found in the conversations he had with Kat. Our calls continued as scheduled, twice weekly for 10-15 minutes each call. There were weeks that Dad wouldn't call, and he would follow up as soon as possible to tell me how they were not allowed out of their cells for the one hour.

February 2021 — Kat was preparing to file — after all the long hours of getting the information from Montana and Oklahoma, as well as from North Carolina.

March 12, 2021: No call from Dad in eleven days. The scheduled calls didn't happen, despite me holding my breath at 5 p.m. on Mondays and Wednesdays. Nothing. I recall this date often, recalling each moment of March 12, 2021. It was a great day, a day planned with family, our annual Spring Break trip, although this year was different. Due to COVID, our cruise was canceled, so we decided to rent an Airbnb in Ft. Lauderdale, Florida for the week. It never was far from my mind that I hadn't heard from Dad, and I planned to call the prison when I arrived in Florida to touch base. While at Chicago O'Hare, Ava and I got in line at a pizza shop, before boarding our flight. In line, my phone rang. *Unknown Caller.* I answered right away to the most horrifying call of my life.

Dad was on the other end gasping for air. I could not understand the words he was attempting to say. Gasping, gulping, fighting for every breath... I heard "scared". I heard "help." He was breathless, he was crying. I said, "Daddy what's wrong, what's wrong Daddy?" I handed Ava the phone, "Can you understand Grandpa?" Ava was in shock, she couldn't understand and in fear said, "Mom what's wrong — what's wrong?" as she handed the phone back. I fell to the ground right there in the line for pizza. Dad had always taught me to pray in moments of fear. I immediately began to pray, loudly, over Dad. I asked for Jesus to be near, hold my daddy, give him breath in his lungs... NOW LORD.... TOUCH LORD!!! I told Dad to go to the officers and tell them he couldn't breathe. He was able to get some words out, he said he had been in the hole again, COVID. That was all I heard. All that I could understand. I assured Dad at this moment, I am fighting for you, I will call everyone, the prison, the senators, and Kat. As the call ended, my heart was beating, pounding, I could hear every beat in my face and in my chest. "Daddy, go to them, ask for help. I am fighting, Dad. I am here. I will not stop. I love YOU."

The phone disconnected and I stood up and walked out of the line as people stared. I didn't care, they had no idea the call that I just had. They didn't know my daddy was in a unit within a Federal Prison, a unit that kept him locked up 24-hours a day in a 7x10 cell. They didn't know and I didn't care. Tears flowing, I was now gasping for breath. I ran to my mom. She was frightened, what was wrong? I explained the phone call, Ava shared her experience. My brain was running a million miles a minute. *Who do I call?* Kat. Call Kat. I did and left her a detailed message about the phone call I had just had. I called the prison and was directed from the receptionist to Dad's counselor. No answer, I left a message. I called back to the prison and explained to the reception desk the phone call I just had. I was told there was nobody available to talk to me, I cried, I pleaded with the officer to help. Again, the answer was the same, "I can send you to his counselor." All of these calls, all of these tears, all of the left messages while sitting at a departure gate on a Thursday afternoon at Chicago O'Hare airport. It was time to board the plane. I wanted to run to a plane that would take me to Indiana, however I knew there would be nothing I could do once I landed. I boarded the plane.

Friday, in Ft Lauderdale, I continued to call the prison, and was always directed to Dad's counselor. Message after message, I pleaded for someone to just let me know my dad was alive. Many conversations with Mom, as we concluded he must have COVID due to his lack of breath, the gasping for air and somewhere in our conversation he had said COVID. Kat called and I explained the call to her and the lack of help from the prison. Kat, in her compassion and empathy, agreed to attempt to reach Dad as well.

Saturday, Sunday, despite it being the weekend, and being on vacation, I could not think of anything but Dad. Wondering if he was still alive crossed my mind more times than I could count. *Did he die, alone in a cell, afraid, crying out to someone for help as he did on the phone?*

Monday, March 16, I awoke and phoned the prison. No answer. Mid-morning, while driving to South Beach, my phone rang as *Terre Haute* came up on my screen. I answered before the words Terre Haute even registered in my brain. "Hell, he, hello." I could hardly speak fast enough. I immediately pulled into a Walgreens parking lot; I didn't know what I would hear. On the other end of the line a man introduced himself as Mr. Rory, the Unit Manager of the CMU unit. He was kind, he was calm and began to explain there had been a medical emergency with my father and he had been taken to a hospital. He noted that due to security, however, he could not tell me if Dad was still in the hospital, or if he had been brought back to the institution. I asked a lot of questions, "Does he have COVID? Is he on a ventilator? Is he breathing?"

COMPASSIONATE RELEASE - IS THERE COMPASSION?

Mr. Rory could only tell me there was a medical emergency and someone would be reaching out to me within the next 24-hours. While I understood the security aspect, I could not understand the lack of compassion for the security policy. I did not blame Mr. Rory, I understood the fine line of his position, and I understood policy. It didn't help, however. Mr. Rory and I had further conversation and our call ended.

I called Mom, who was back at the Airbnb. I called Dad's sister. I called Kat. I called my best friend. I was literally dying inside. While so thankful for the call, I was left with so many unanswered questions, the pain, the physical pain was almost too much to bear. The scenarios that ran through my head, the endless scenarios. The thought of Dad possibly being in the hospital, was he even awake? I was so thankful to know he had help or was possibly out of the CMU and in a hospital bed. I did not know.

The following day, March 17, my cousins had scheduled a time to parasail. We all went over to Ft. Lauderdale beach. I stood with my Aunt Heather and Uncle Kevin, while my children dove into the waves. This was my place; it has always been my place. Ft. Lauderdale beach, feeling the waves crash over my feet. I didn't get in because I couldn't set my phone down. It stayed in my hand just in case I received a call.

My cousins were flying in front of us with all of us waving. As the sun was shining, with the smell of the ocean water, and the sand between my toes, my phone rang. Terre Haute—I could barely swipe to answer the call. My hands were shaking with fear of the unknown. *What would I hear, do I want to know?*

"Amy, this is Mrs. Eisley, I am your Dad's counselor, he is next to me and would like to talk to you. I will let you know he is currently in the hospital; however, we ask that you do not share this publicly. Oh Jesus, HE IS ALIVE. HE IS OUT OF THE CMU AND HE CAN TALK TO ME. "Yes, yes. I understand. Oh, thank you, thank you." Mrs. Eisley handed Dad the phone, and I heard a voice—a voice I did not recognize. Although it wasn't the same voice I heard five days prior, it was Dad. His exact words, "Amy, I have cancer. It started in my kidney, moved to my lungs and my brain."

The world stopped. The waves crashed against me, as I now lay in the water. I had slowly fallen to my knees, and everything was in slow motion. I wanted to scream, but something told me not to, only for Dad's sake. I repeated Dad's words, my Aunt, next to me, just held me as I fought off every emotion. The waves crashing, "Oh Dad, oh Dad, it's ok, it's ok. We will fight this. We will get you home and fight this." Tears, shaking, I continued to ask Dad questions. "Are you comfortable Daddy? What have they done, what have they discussed with you?"

Dad shared, with a very, very slow-paced conversation. "I am in a bed with a lot of pillows, it is nice, so nice. They are taking care of me. This bed feels like heaven." He went on to share, with his very slow, very different voice. My son, Ben, took the phone and walked along the water talking to Grandpa. My Uncle Kevin then took the phone and shared a story with Dad about an old Mustang Dad used to have. There were laughs. I sat. I was hugged, and cared for by my aunt, she did not leave my side. I cried; I had the "gut hurt cry." *Oh Lord, why?*

I got the phone back and Dad shared that he thought he was going to die in a cell, a cell with a dirt floor, where he was put due to suspicion of him having COVID. He described the cell as being in the back of the CMU unit, and the dirt floor. He shared he could not stand, he could not button his clothes, he could not feed himself, and he had been wetting himself. He shared that after our call last Thursday, he was left there, and he was able to have a friend communicate via email with Kat. He shared how despite this diagnosis, Jesus was in control. *Oh, how he was comforting my heart in the midst of this devastating news.*

I asked a lot of questions, and assured Dad, I would be calling Kat as soon as our phone call ended. He was so thankful. He never wavered from his strong faith, of just who was in control. It poured out of him, with every word. I told Dad I was so proud of him, for his bravery, for planting the seeds of the love of Jesus in me and that no matter what, we would get through this. We prayed together and he was told he would still only receive the two calls per week and so we would be talking again on Friday. Shocking. I asked if Dad could call my brother, and Mrs. Eisley said we could split our 15-minute call in half, and she would allow Dad to call Mike too. He was just diagnosed with kidney cancer that had metastasized to his lungs and brain, and we still get the two fifteen-minute calls. We were on speaker phone, and I asked if I could come to the hospital, and the counselor said at this time that was not an option, but she would see what they could do.

I would take what I could get. After the call, I was stuck. Stuck half in the ocean, while sand and water rushed over me. "Lord, I need you to direct my path, direct Kat's path, and keep my daddy comfortable." We were in for the fight of our lives. I just needed him to come home and spend his last days with me and my children. That is all. My heart hurt, worse than ever and I immediately called Kat. She felt my pain. She empathized with my pain. She assured me she would add this to the Compassionate Release motion and get it filed immediately.

4:30 p.m. — I received an email. The *Compassionate Release* was filed with the Federal Court in Raleigh, North Carolina. The judge gave the government fourteen days to file their response — this is how the process works. After they file their response, Kat will have an opportunity to respond, and it will go before the judge for a ruling.

In the following days, medical records were subpoenaed from the prison and the hospital. I reviewed all of these, as did those close to me. One of my dearest friends, Jessica, who is in the medical field, would explain all the medical language that I did not understand. Every day there were updates. I learned Dad was not taken out of the hole until Monday, March 15, which meant after that horrific phone call, he stayed in that hell hole another four days. I learned Dad's official diagnosis. Renal Cell Carcinoma with metastasis to his lungs and brain. Treatment was urgent, and Dad was never a fan of chemotherapy. We had several conversations about this over the years and Dad firmly believed chemotherapy was not the answer to curing cancer, in fact, he believed it was dangerous. I looked forward to our next call, as I began researching everything I was learning. What stood out to me the most in my research was, "terminal."

Dad now had a terminal illness. The requirements of *Compassionate Release:* Age, at least sixty-five years old; is experiencing a serious deterioration in physical or mental health due to age and have served at least ten years or 75% of the sentence, whichever is less. Dad met them all—each and every one of the requirements for release. My brain began to prepare for him to come home.

Another phone call on Friday, March 19, the call now registered Terre Haute on my screen. I was relaxing at my Airbnb by the pool. Dad's counselor was on the phone. She was kind, and eager to share Dad was waiting patiently to talk to me. I could hear her telling him she was setting the phone to "speaker" and placing the phone on his chest. "Hi Daddy!" I couldn't wait to share that his Compassionate Release request had been filed. Dad shared, he already knew this and how excited he was. He shared Kat had been able to speak with him and she had been walking him through the process. Praise Jesus! For just a moment, we could only see the end result, the reunion. Not the terminal illness or the fact that he was there, needing me, and I could not be there. For just that moment, we were looking at the future, then back to reality. Dad shared he had been able to keep some food down, he was feeling "ok" but so excited to be sleeping in a regular bed, despite being shackled to the bed by his left ankle.

Wait. What? I didn't let Dad know how much this bothered me. He went on to share that an intern was coming to "take him for a walk, even though he couldn't walk but only two steps." This brought him to tears. He described the intern as a young woman learning the ropes, she was kind, she was gentle and treated him like a "patient" not as an inmate. This touched his heart.

We talked about the doctor's thoughts, and how they brought up chemotherapy. Dad declined this and shared he even tried to fill the doctor's in on the dangers of chemo. We laughed. Dad shared that one of his doctors brought up immunotherapy. I told him I would research this, but from what I knew, it was new and less invasive. I told him I would join him in prayer for clear and specific answers. He was also on pain meds, I could hear the weakness in his voice, yet so full of temporary energy to hear my voice over the speaker phone. I told Dad I had been in contact with Kat as well, and we were waiting on the government's response, and then the judge would make his decision. We prayed over this, we prayed for the judge. I never told Dad I was on vacation, this seemed so unfair. We planned our next call for the following Monday, and I assured him I would be in prayer, along with so many others.

I contacted the prison to see who I could talk to about visiting Dad upon my return. As the daily updates from the hospital continued to flood my email, I knew we didn't have long. I was connected with the attorney over the CMU and Death Row. To my surprise, she had also filed a *Compassionate Release* for Dad. She had been in contact with Kat as well and shared that our filing would probably be a faster route, but she had submitted hers to the warden as well. This gave me such comfort.

Our conversations were lengthy, and she shared how she didn't really know Dad personally because he had never been a problem. We laughed and shared stories. I shared with her my dad's strong beliefs in an unjust system, and his faithfulness to Jesus through it all. I shared his love for fishing, and his three most loved things in the world. Jesus, his kids and grandchildren, and America.

Courts, filings, suspended documents, were part of my daily life. Daily opening court documents, the waiting was excruciating.

I needed to see my dad.

CHAPTER 9

The Parking Lot

I returned home and could not sit still. It was hard to think, it was frustrating to sit and wait for the next call. I decided to go to Terre Haute. My best friend, Angie, Ava, and I packed up and went directly to the hospital. Although I knew I could not get in, it was important for me to be nearby. Before even checking into a hotel, we sat in a parking lot, facing the hospital. It was nighttime, and the hospital was lit up. We played Dad's favorite music—Dan Fogelberg, Neil Diamond and several worship songs. There was comfort in knowing he was so close, closer than he had been in so long. We cried, we bawled, we sat in silence. The frustration and agony of knowing my dying father was somewhere in this large building was near torture. I just needed to be near him.

We checked into our hotel, and I felt some small comfort that I was less than a mile away. I only wished Dad knew. The time went so slow. I contacted the prison the next morning, and left messages for Dad's counselor to call me with any updates. After several calls that day, I was able to speak with her and shared with her that I was in Terre Haute, staying in a hotel. I asked if there was someone I would need to talk to in order to possibly set up a visit. She shared she had been working on this and would do her best to get something set up.

I continued to work remotely and found it ever so difficult to focus. Angie and Ava kept my spirits up, we even had a pillow fight one evening. It was hard to laugh, hard to smile, and hard to get out of bed.

A call was scheduled with Dad at noon. The time went past 12:15, 12:30, 12:45 and no call. I called Mom—I was terrified something had happened. Finally, at 1:00 p.m., Terre Haute was calling. I answered to Dad's counselor, Mrs. Eisley, apologizing for the late call. For a second I could breathe, he was still okay. She gave the phone to Dad, and he was weaker than ever. I filled him in on what I had learned about immunotherapy and told him I thought it was a good idea, noting that we would continue this when he came home. He agreed and said he had started it. He said he was in pain, he was sick and in between horrific, deep coughs, he would tell me he was okay. He would fall asleep mid-sentence, and I would just listen to him breathe, while in my mind putting myself in a chair next to him, holding his hand, or lying next to him, just touching. He asked about the *Compassionate Release* in between nodding off, I told him we were still waiting on the response from the government. He would say, "In God's time." Yes Dad, in God's time. This phone call was rough. It took all of my strength not to cry and lose it every second of that call. I was able to tell Dad I was in Terre Haute, in fact, I was right down the street at a hotel. Dad was elated, although his elation was soft, and he thanked me over and over again. "I am here Daddy, and I'm not leaving without you, I am trying to get in for a visit." He said he was hoping for the same, he was praying for the same and believed it would happen. We prayed together and he drifted off to sleep. Our call ended.

Angie, Ava, and I spent another evening in the parking lot. Praying, and worshipping, asking God for our specific needs and wants. "Lord, let Dad be released. Just give me time to get him home. Lord, let him ride the six hours in the front seat of the car, let him feel the wind in his face, see the sky, the trees, the lakes. Lord, let him see my children and of course, Penny." Time in silence, time of reflection, of memories we had of Dad as little girls. The Lord gave us laughter in these moments of reflection. I just knew we would be bringing him; we were on the right track.

The next morning, I received a phone call from Mrs. Eisley. I was going to be allowed a visit with Dad the following day at 12:30 p.m. I would be given two hours. I shared my gratitude with Mrs. Eisley. "Oh thank you Jesus!" It had been so long, one contact visit in June of 2019, and it had been 11 years prior to that. I could not wait; I could not contain the joy in my heart. Mike was also given a visit, but it would have to be the following day, we could only go in one at a time.

On a phone call with Dad, I was able to share that I was coming the next day. It was a Thursday, and he was weaker on each and every call. I told him I was coming and that, "I can hardly stand the wait." Dad replied, "I know. I know." Between tears, his weakness and fatigue made it difficult to finish the call. I asked Dad if he was in pain, "No, not really." I asked, "Can you hold on Daddy, do you think you can hold on?" Between coughs, gently he said, "Yes sweet pea, yes." "A few more days Dad, just a few and we will have our response from the judge, I will be bringing you home." "Yes sweet pea."

I immediately called Mike and shared the good news. For Mike this was different. He had not seen dad in over twenty years, as a young teenager when we went to El Reno. Mike had spoken to Dad over the years but his relationship with Dad was very different from mine, which I understood. Mike was thankful for this opportunity and said he would head to Terre Haute. Mike had some amends to make with Dad and felt the compelling need to tell Dad of his forgiveness at how things turned out, and how much he turned out to look like Dad and share so many similar mannerisms. This was important for Mike, and so very important for Dad.

The next morning, I woke up, and could hardly gather my composure. Angie and Ava prayed with me, and off I went to the hospital. Before going in I made a video of myself, distraught in my face, in my voice. I was going in.

As I entered the door I was directed to a lady dressed in uniform, who was walking toward me. She introduced herself as Mrs. Eisley. After so many conversations over the phone, it was a blessing to put a face with a name. We started to walk, a long walk, and up an elevator, where we came to double doors while talking about Dad. She said he was better today and so anxious for our visit. Oh, how I knew the feeling.

The doors were opened and on the other side, a man stood wearing a Department of Justice coat. He asked me to take everything out of my pockets and give him my keys and phone. Mrs. Eisley then led me around a corner to a long hallway, where I could clearly see two Correctional Officers standing outside a door. I stopped for a second. I had to breathe and take in the moment. "Just breathe Amy. Lord be near, give me strength in every step, give my daddy strength." Mrs. Eisley was understanding, and said, "Whenever you're ready." "I'm ready."

My legs walked unconsciously, as I began to walk faster and faster. I came to the room where the two officers were standing and walked into the room. No, I ran, I actually ran to Dad. I ran to his bedside, climbed up on the side of the bed with my knee barely balancing me, as I hugged him. He was frail, very frail, he was crying, I was sobbing. *Oh, to touch you Daddy*—the comfort this brought my soul. Mrs. Eisley sat in a recliner in the corner of the room. Dad was propped up with lots of pillows, which he loved. We held hands, I rubbed his arm as I sat down in the chair next to him. The tears were falling, there was not a shut-off button. We just talked. We talked about my kids, the weather, the immunotherapy, the hope we had for his release, Compassionate Release and meeting all the requirements, Kat, and how thankful we were for her taking his case. So much to talk about, and a clock that ran faster than normal. Every second was precious. Just to look into my dad's eyes, not in an inmate uniform, not behind glass, he was here in front of me. Dad was frustrated with the "leg iron" as he called it, his left ankle chained to the bed. He shared this made it hard to turn, but he was sure to add, "I'm not complaining."

Mrs. Eisley stepped out of the room and came back asking if it was okay for the prison Chaplain to join us momentarily. "Oh yes" Dad said, as I agreed, "Yes please!" In walked a young man as Dad was smiling ear to ear. The man introduced himself as Mr. Wood, and he began to share stories of Dad's faithfulness, of his feelings of inadequacy when it came to Dad with his knowledge and faith that surpassed all understanding. He shared of Dad, sometimes being the only person on Saturdays coming to a worship service. Dad was always there if allowed. Mr. Wood was in awe of Dad's relationship with Jesus, despite the circumstances. We laughed as Mr. Wood shared of Dad changing the guitar strings to, "better match his voice." Dad was not shy to say he had in fact done this many times. We then were allowed to have communion together. This was important to both of us, but Mr. Wood may not have known that I was just a little girl the last time we were able to share this sacred event. Jesus was present. I could feel Him.

Mr. Wood said his goodbyes, and assured Dad and I that he would be checking on Dad frequently. He was empathetic, and it was obvious of his belief in Hebrews 13:3. He not only remembered those in prison, but he lived it and breathed it. Dad was always so thankful for this man. He had shared over the last couple of years, different stories of Mr. Wood and his kindness.

We continued to share, I continued to hold Dad's hand. Our two hours flew by, and I was told it was time to end our visit. I felt an overwhelming peace out of nowhere, an indescribable peace. The Lord told me in this moment, "This is not the end, this is not the last time Amy, you are not saying goodbye." While I wasn't sure if that meant in this world, or if it meant I would see him again in heaven, I was okay. Being "okay" didn't stop the tears from falling from our eyes, but we hugged as the officers and nurse began unplugging dad's IV from the wall and unlocking the brakes on his bed. Dad and I prayed together, holding hands. I assured him, I would continue working night and day and most importantly, I would be back to pick him up. He found comfort in the fact I was staying down the road, and I made sure he knew I would be near, praying in the parking lot each night. They began to wheel Dad out in front of me, I walked slowly behind him with Mrs. Eisley. I kissed him again on the forehead as he turned a corner one way, and I went back out the double doors.

Once in my car, I cried. I called Mom, and shared the visit, the two hours I was so honored to spend with Dad. I called Mike and told him how wonderful it was to just be next to him. Mike was on his way for his visit the next day, (Friday) and I returned to the hotel. While driving, I spoke to my Father, I asked for Dad to be able to come home, I asked for continued strength. I asked for a miracle.

That evening Ava and I went out for supper. We had crab legs,

THE PARKING LOT

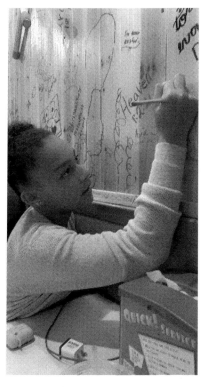

our favorite. In the restaurant, guests were allowed to write on the wooden walls. Ava wrote to Grandpa, "Ava was here, I love you Grandpa." My heart again, crushed. I, too, took the opportunity to write to Dad on the wall. "Daddy we are here, I love you. Russell D. Landers 2021.

Mike arrived late that night and was up early for his visit. My sister-in-law, Angie, and I waited patiently in the parking lot. So many discussions of what was next, will we have time to get him home, is he strong enough. Again, time flew by and soon Mike was walking out of the hospital. Mike shared with us being able to help Dad eat his soup, and how when he first entered the room, Dad thought he was our grandfather, Ardean. They laughed and Dad could not believe the amazing man Mike had grown into. The years of being apart led them back to that moment, there in a hospital room, in an undisclosed area, with officers and a counselor in the chair, over two decades later. Mike was at peace. He shared that their conversations were about his children, and just life. Mike had hoped that Dad would come home, if only for a short time, to continue to catch up on the last twenty plus years.

Angie, Ava, and I stayed and continued to follow all of the daily updates from Kat. The hospital records continued to come in and Dad was stable for the most part. The updates included daily documentation, from each shift, and an overview of his vitals. Reading over the chart, the notes would repeatedly say, "Federal prisoner here with progressive symptoms." That always stood out. *"Left side facial droop, he reports it was called Bell's palsy. Symptoms worsening, left sided weakness, cannot read and is having difficulty with comprehension. HIH as above. Symptoms began 2 weeks ago so he is not in the window for TPA or mechanical thrombectomy. CT head reviewed with Dr. N and Dr. S, concern for metastatic brain lesion with vasogenic edema. Dr. S agrees to consult Dr. K accepts admission. Patient will require work up for primary cancer.*

That Sunday, we decided to come home for a day or two. My next scheduled call with Dad would be on Wednesday, April 7. That was such a long time, but I stayed in contact with the prison attorney, and Mrs. Eisley, who assured me they would be in contact if something were to happen.

Monday, April 5, Kat called, and the government had asked for an extension "due to the complexities of Dad's case." The judge denied the extension. This was great news. Kat explained the judge ordered the response to be turned in immediately. Kat said she would share this with me once it was submitted, but to be cautious, they "are always very ugly and they do their best to state every reason a person shouldn't be released." Kat said she would be responding right away once submitted and the judge would then make a ruling. She asked if I had been able to talk to a doctor, to which I told her I had tried and was always denied. She asked that I call the prison and speak with someone about setting this up right away. Kat was so smart, so driven, covering every base. She wanted to hear from a doctor, so she could add this to her response.

I received the *Compassionate Release* response. I was broken. I had to remember what Kat told me, "It will be ugly. The purpose of the response is to give every reason your dad should not get out. This is normal, they do this with every Compassionate Release response." I prepared myself, prepared my heart, although it didn't do any good. The response was harsh, there were untrue statements. A picture was painted of a "terrorist." "Attack, violent." The words used to describe Dad were false. There was never an "attack" there was never "violence." *(See his charges)* "Continued threat he poses..." He could hardly see, hardly walk, was sometimes even unresponsive. "Poses too great of a threat to the public." How can a blind, bed-ridden man who has cancer in his kidneys, lungs, and brain pose a threat to the public? This was about me, not even about Dad anymore, he was transitioning. I swallowed it, and still have my opinion to the lack of truth, and persuasive statements made in this document.

Each day, so very difficult to not have answers, not to have updates, except from a document that was uploaded into the court tracker. So many questions every hour of every day. I could not just call the hospital, it wasn't allowed. I just wanted to know how my daddy was, and this was not allowed

I was able to speak with the prison attorney, who said she would have the doctor working with Dad call me on Tuesday, April 6 at noon.

Tuesday, working from home, I scheduled my lunch for noon, to accept the call. I also decided to record the call, just so I didn't miss anything that Kat would need for her update to the court. The doctor called timely, noon exactly. I answered, not knowing the words he was about to speak. "Your Dad is not doing well at all; his lesions are getting worse. He had a seizure last night and is not responding."

Stop.

Breathe.

Gasp.

Wait, time stops. Wait.

No.

He continued to share that Dad had been unresponsive since last evening. Dad had a seizure and hadn't woken up. I asked questions, I yelled for my son Ben to come listen to the call. I asked, "If a judge were to rule tomorrow for his release, will I be able to bring him home?" The doctor, conferring with his nurse, "No I don't believe so, we are beyond that." OH GOD. NO. NO. NO. "Can I come to him, PLEASE, can I come to him?" The doctor asked the nurse if I could come, and they responded with, "You will need to talk to the prison." My mind was going a million miles a minute, horrified, this cannot be happening, I will call the prison, I will come, not listening anymore to the call. The doctor noted, "I have one final question, God forbid his heart stops, do you want him on a breathing machine?" Dear GOD, what WAS I HEARING. How do I answer that, "Ben, do we want him on a breathing machine?" Ben replied "Yes, until you get there." I relayed the message to the doctor. Our call ended, my phone recording did not.

I've replayed the recording and know it well. The horrific cries, yelling, even cursing. "We almost had him home and he's dying right now." The gut-wrenching yells of a daughter who believed with everything I had, that I would have a few days, maybe even just a week to love on my daddy for just a little while longer. "Get my mom, get my mom" screams. Ben dialing my mom, "He's dying, I have to go, I have to go."

Mom, in pure utter disbelief, "Amy what is wrong?" It was hard to understand me, it was hard for me to understand me. Just

THE PARKING LOT

get me to him. I called Jessica, my dear friend to tell her what the doctor had said, "Jess he's dying right now, he's dying." Mom was calling back asking if I wanted her to call Mike. "I don't care, I don't care, just get me to him." I ended the call. Ben was doing everything he could to stop the madness, the screaming, the curdling screams. "He's still breathing Mom, he's still alive." I ran to my room and grabbed a handful of clothes out of my dirty clothes basket, threw them in a bag, no thought, pure emotion. I ran up the stairs and to the garage to find my mom and brother pulling in. Mike, "Let's go." Mommy, oh Mommy, make this pain go away, as she grabbed me, my knees literally buckled as I put all of my weight onto her. "I can't do this, I almost had him home."

Mike and I jumped in the car, off we went. Mom stayed back for my children, and soon after we were on the road I had a voice mail come through on my phone from Mr. Rory. He stated, "I understand you're in route to Terre Haute. Could you please call and let me know your arrival time, I will meet you at the hospital." How did he know? The doctors must have reached out. Thank God. I read it to Mike, who immediately called him back. He explained the phone call with the doctor, that I was inconsolable, and just needing to see him. Our GPS indicated a 9:30 p.m. arrival time. Mr. Rory was in that moment the key to me seeing Dad one last time, unless, unless the *Compassionate Release* goes through in the next day or two, and I can have Dad moved to the regular part of the hospital where I can lay with him, hold his hand, and he will not die alone. Alone, like he has been for over twenty-four years. "Please God." Mr. Rory would meet us at the hospital at 9:30. We were directed to the same entrance I had used only six days prior.

Driving. Mike and I love music, particularly 80's music. He found solace in trying to laugh and sing along. I tried to no avail.

I watched out the window. I was in shock. I was not going to say goodbye to my daddy. A nightmare. I was in the middle of it. *Could someone please wake me up?* We are so close to a decision. This is NOT FAIR. The drive was what I needed, with just my brother. Though our relationship with Dad was very different, he was Dad to both of us, and we needed to be together. The highway never ended. It was long. Daylight hours turned dark, as we left Iowa into Illinois, and finally signs for Indiana. Signs for Terre Haute. I needed to hear a song, that spoke to my spirit, and Mike obliged to my request. *Praise You in this Storm.* Lord knew the storm I was in, the nightmare. I could only praise Him in the moment. It hurt too bad. Watching the yellow lines, worshipping, yelling to Jesus. Mike drove, drove faster and there was the hospital, the parking lot where I spent so many hours.

We parked and ran to the door. No one was there, so we sat on a bench. Mr. Rory eventually came and guided us to the same long hallway, with the officers standing outside. My hair all over the place, mismatched clothes, we began the walk to Dad's room. Mike walked in first, as I stood talking to the nurse. I asked if he was awake, she said, "No we did a catheter change about an hour ago, with no response. She did note that while they were wheeling Dad in his bed, she yelled, "Russ, Amy & Mike are here." Out of nowhere Dad replied "Good," and went back to sleep.

I walked into the low-lit room, just the light over Dad's bed was on. I first saw Mike, standing at the end of Dad's bed, his mouth open, as if in utter disbelief. He turned to me, and without saying it, he was scared for me to see Dad. My eyes scanned from Mike to Dad. "Oh Daddy." I unconsciously ran to his bed, climbed on the side and laid my head on his chest. His head had been shaved and was turned to the left, while he slowly fought for each breath. My tears came freely, as I said, "Daddy I am here,

I am here Daddy." While holding his face and speaking to him, "Daddy open your eyes, open your eyes Daddy, I am here." Mike, now standing at Dad's bedside, was still. Dad's eyes began to rapidly flicker, and in that moment his left eye opened, while a tear slowly ran down his cheek. I wiped the tear, "I am here Dad, I am here, Mike is here." I could not tell him what my heart so longed to say, that I was taking him home. My soul still cries because I believe this is what he held onto his last bit of strength to hear. I stayed there, holding his face, rubbing his head and in between prayers gave him reminders of my eternal greatness for his steadfast faith.

I asked Mr. Rory, who stood at the end of the bed, if I could play some music for dad. He responded, "Do whatever you need to do." I grabbed my phone, sobbing uncontrollably and began to play *Run for the Roses*, one of Dad's all-time favorite songs, as I sat the phone on his pillow next to his ear. "Born in the valley and raised in the trees of western Kentucky…on wobbly knees…" the tears from Dad's left eye began to fall more rapidly. He did his best to mouth the words of this all-time favorite song that he used to play on his trombone when I was a little girl. As the song ended, a worship song started playing, and loud and clearly Dad said, "Jesus." This would be the last word he spoke. As the song played on, Dad drifted away, and was back asleep. I left my phone playing the music from my playlist titled "Daddy." All his favorites, and some of my favorites too.

Mike began to share stories with Mr. Rory of Dad and ask questions of just how he had lived over the last thirteen years. I laid next to Dad, half on his bed, half on a chair, rubbing his arms, his face and being intentional about being in the moment, my last moments with my daddy. I didn't know how to do this, and nobody could have prepared me. In my heart, I just knew it was too late now to bring him home, so if the judge would grant his *Compassionate Release* in the next day or two, I would have him moved out of the prison unit of the hospital and moved into the regular wing. I would lay with him, share stories with him in his ear, pray with him, worship with him and spend every second with my daddy until he takes his last breath. IF he can hold on that long and IF the judge grants *Compassionate Release*.

An hour passed, it passed so quickly, it felt like only a minute. We were told it was time to end the visit. Lord, how do I do this? *How do I say goodbye Is this the end, will it be the last time I see my daddy in his physical body? We have lost so much time. Can I please have a little more time, please oh please. I can't do this. Someone help me. How? What? I don't know how. Help me. Lord, please help me.*

As these thoughts ran through my mind, it felt as if I were drowning and didn't know how to swim. Slowly, Mike said his goodbyes, he leaned into Dad's ear and told him we were all okay, and it was okay to go home. I could not hear this. I am not ready. Mike then asked, "Can we look at his feet?" Mike had two reasons for asking this question, first to see if Dad's feet were *mottling* which happens right before death. Second, to see if the leg irons were still on his leg. Again, Mr. Rory told us that was fine.

Mike pulled back the blankets to see Dad's feet, with his blue hospital socks. I pulled back his sock, and there was no mottling that we, non-health care people could identify. And there, attached to his left ankle, the leg shackle, connected to his bed. He hated this thing, and in all of my fog of thoughts and emotions, I again lost it. My tears would not stop, I could feel them in the core of my being. I could not understand how we forget the dignity of human beings, even on their deathbed. Again, I knew it was policy, but how and why? He was nonresponsive, and within days of death. I pulled his sock back up, rubbed his feet, as I closed my eyes remembering when Jesus washed the feet of the twelve disciples at the Last Supper. *John 13:1-15*. Although, I wasn't washing Dad's feet, in my mind, I was. Dad had already inherited the Kingdom of God; I knew this to be a fact.

I then went back to the side of Dad's bed and continued praying loudly over him. The room was quiet, a stillness in the air. In that prayer, I still asked Jesus to open the door for Dad's release and repeated, "Oh how we trust you, Jesus." I kissed his forehead, his hand, and his cheek as I turned to follow Mike out the door. As I stepped into the doorway of the hospital room, my natural reaction to turn back to him took over. All of the times in our lives, I just ran back for one more. In Raleigh when at the airport, in each of the prisons, my visit just six days prior, always just one more, just…one…more. One more touch. Every time I left him, these words played through my mind. Another kiss, and I tried to walk away again. As I got to the door, out of the corner of my eye, I noticed tears in one of the officer's eyes as we made eye contact through the tears. I ran back…just one more time.

Mike and I spent a few minutes talking to the nurse and the staff. The nurse was kind, and assured me that if Dad passed, someone would be with him. I pleaded with her, "Please, could someone just hold his hand if I can't be there." She said they would do their best. Mike and I were escorted out as we thanked Mr. Rory for coming into work late that evening and allowing our visit. We also asked that he pass on to others who were involved in making the decision to allow us our visit, how thankful we were.

Goodbye Daddy, I am still fighting.

1000 GIFTS FROM A 7 X 10

CHAPTER 10

Compassion

Mike and I stayed in Terre Haute that night after leaving Dad. We sat in our hotel room, with some shock at how quick he went from talking to us the week before to using his very last strength to open his eyes, try and mouth words, and speak loud and clearly, "Jesus" before going back to sleep. We shared our memories as children, and our perceptions of Dad, and the life he lived. We spoke of the loneliness, shame, separation anxiety, sadness and anger over the last twenty-four and a half years. We stayed up half the night, knowing the judge would be deciding in the next day or two.

I woke up to my phone ringing. *North Carolina—Kat*. I answered immediately. Kat, whom I had been communicating with several times a day, wanted to know how the visit went. I shared with her how difficult it was and at this point, I would not be able to bring him home, but would instead share his last days and hours with him in the hospital if he were to be released. Kat shared she was continuing to update the courts and had asked for the court to expedite the decision based on Dad's decline. Kat believed the judge would be deciding on this day.

Kat explained to me the approximate six-hour process once *Compassionate Release* was granted and asked that I should stay in

Terre Haute. She assured me she would do her best to move the process along as quickly as possible, but that I should be there. I assured her I wasn't going anywhere. Kat informed me she would be going into court this morning, and if anything came through, her secretary would email me right away.

I called and spoke with the attorney at the institution to see where they were with the *Compassionate Release* they had filed. Katherine was doing her very best to expedite the process, however it still took time. I shared with her where we were in our process, and that we believed the judge would be deciding today. She too, spoke of the lengthy process once granted, however, noted she too would do her best to expedite the process. She even noted she had the case pulled up, documents were being entered, and the paperwork on her end had been started. She could see the documents being entered by the courts in real time.

Mike decided he would run home quickly but would return after taking care of some things at work and home. We went to rent a vehicle for me, as true to my word, I was not going anywhere. I will wait. Wait for the answer. I will wait for the release of my dad, at this point, even though he may not be aware. I would have the closure that every daughter needs when her daddy is going "home."

We arrived the car rental at approximately 9:00 a.m. As always, my phone stayed glued to my hand and alerted me I had a new email as I reached to open the door.

"Mike. This is it!"

"Mike, Mike, it's from Kat's secretary. Oh, my goodness MIKE, he made a decision." I let go of the door and stood facing Mike, as I tapped my phone to open the email.

April 7, 2022

"I am recusing myself from the case. I am ordering a new judge to oversee this case."

As I read this allowed, my knees buckled and I collapsed, right there in the car rental entryway.

Time stopped.

My brain could not contain what I had just read. *You can't do that? You made decisions on this case for a month. This can't happen. How can this happen? He's dying, we don't have time.* The thoughts that ran through my brain. *I cannot. I cannot. I don't know what to do.* As I looked up at my brother in utter disbelief, he responded, "Amy, it's ok, it's ok. I don't understand either, I don't, I just don't. Come on Amy, let's wait for Kat to call."

As I stood up, my body felt as if my soul had just left my body. *This was for me; I didn't do anything. Why are you taking this from me? What do I do? How do I take my next breath? Daddy, oh Daddy, I don't know what to do… I just need to talk to you…Lord what? How does this happen?*

Mike held me as we walked back to his car. We just sat—sat and processed the injustice of what had just happened. My phone rang and Kat was on the other end. I could hear the utter disbelief, the shock and disappointment in her voice. "Amy, I am so sorry, I just don't know, I don't understand, I don't even know what to say," as I could hear the tears in her voice. We spoke briefly and she stated that as soon as she returned to her office she would file a demand for a new judge to be appointed immediately, and a decision be expedited. Her fight gave me strength, hope, and I am eternally grateful for her. I just knew it was too late.

Mike talked me into driving home. We drove back by the hospital, and both stared, with tears in our eyes as we said goodbye to the air, hoping Dad somehow, someway could feel us. We continued to process our feelings. *It would have been better if he just said "no." How can this happen?*

During the long drive home, our usual joyful, silly energetic beings were somber and frozen in disbelief during the entire six-hour car ride home.

I knew where to shift my hurt—to Jesus. Over the next couple of days, I began to pray for Dad's transition, that although I am not there, Jesus would be near, and Dad would know I did my best. He would transition knowing I fought until the end, and that ultimately he would be free, something he and I had wanted and prayed for day and night for over two decades.

Saturday, April 10, I took Ava to stay with some of my best friends, Chrissy & Zaria, who would take her to her state volleyball tournament, as I could not. I knew I could be getting a call at any time and had been finding solace in laying in my bed, curled in a ball, listening to worship music since I returned home Thursday. Ben rode along, and we left Ava after a brief visit, sharing my pain through every word I spoke. Ben and I had just began driving when my phone rang.

Terre Haute.

I knew what this call was. I pulled into a parking lot, reached over and grabbed Ben's hand and answered the call.

"Hello Amy, This is Officer so & so. I am calling to inform you that your father, Russell Landers, passed away at 12:21 p.m. We are so sorry for your loss. Mr. Landers listed you as the person to send his belongings to, and they will arrive in the next couple of weeks. Again, we are so very sorry for your loss."

Stillness.

"Ok, ok. Thank you."

The tears piled behind my eyes; I hung up the phone. I couldn't breathe. So gently through my labored breaths, my gut tearing apart, the Lord spoke to me and reminded me, "He is free. No more shackles, no more prison bars, Amy he is free."

"Oh Jesus, your kindness and constant comfort in one of the worst moments of my life. Thank you for this reminder." Jesus continued to pour out his love and grace, as Ben switched seats with me, and we began to drive home. I called family and friends and shared my dad's passing and there was a constant theme of those who loved me and those who loved Dad because they loved me... "Amy, he is with Jesus." This I was sure of.

When I arrived home, Mom and I began to read the last update from the hospital. This was my reality, Dad dying on paper, reading the notes that had been updated by each shift every day he was hospitalized. I would always forward the daily updates to Jessica, as she understood the medical terminology and would translate" those terms I did not understand. What I found to be strange, as did Mom and Jessica, was the fact that there were no shift updates from Friday at 7:00 a.m. until his death on Saturday at noon, no shift notes. There was not a missing page, they were numbered. *"Did he die alone?" Does anyone deserve to die like this, alone? Does a daughter deserve to live with this question for the rest of my life?* I could not call and ask the many questions I had, that we all had. Again, I could not call the hospital directly. This will stick with me the remainder of my days.

The tears continued to flow. Dad was free AND HE WAS HOME. He didn't get to experience justice on earth, but his legacy has and will. He is victorious.

1000 GIFTS FROM A 7 X 10

CHAPTER 11

Dad Came Home

Dad was gone and now I had to decide what to do. Knowing he had been away from the area for over twenty-five years, if I had a funeral, would anyone come?

Here's what I did know.

Through the past seven years, Dad and I had many conversations about *Hope City Church* in Waterloo, Iowa. My home church that only seven years prior I played a small role in planting with my best friend Angie and her husband, Pastor Q, Quovadis Marshall. Paster Q had a vision of planting this church prior to his incarceration, and over the years, *Hope City* has become the fastest growing church in Iowa's history. Pastor Q's knowledge and involvement with prison reform and the justice system has become a lifestyle for him. Dad longed to come to *Hope City*.

After many conversations with the prison staff, they informed me of my three options. 1. Have dad cremated and sent to me. 2. Have Dad buried at the prison cemetery. 3. They would fly Dad home.

This was not a difficult decision. I am bringing Dad home. I knew no matter what it took, I was bringing him home.

The prison staff coordinated with the local funeral home. Pastor Q, Mike and I met with the funeral director and shared our wishes. They were kind and had compassion for this unique situation.

Dad arrived home on Friday, April 16, 2021, over two decades since he was last in Waterloo. The funeral home allowed me to visit Dad, and I raced to him. Angie, Jessica, her husband Red, and Ava met me there. We walked in together and were greeted by the funeral director. He shared with me he had a little work to do on Dad, but for the most part, he was ready.

We walked through the double doors, and there at the front of a small service room, in a gray casket, laid my daddy. I nearly fell as my feet stumbled over each other. In a suit, in stillness, laid my daddy, the shell of his being, the hands that protected me, the smile that lit up my world as a little girl. I stood over him, took some pictures of our hands together and just stood or sat in stillness. I noticed the ink still on his thumb, from his *death picture,* which I learned is part of the process when an inmate dies.

I received several messages on Facebook from people I did not know. One from a retired teacher, who worked for years in prison. She had heard of Dad's passing and wanted to share with me how he impacted the lives of so many while he was incarcerated. She noted, she only knew how to find me because of the endless stories Dad told of me, and his family, this is how she knew my name. Dad taught so many inmates to read, and the impact this had on their lives. She shared his patience and how he was smiling, always smiling.

Another message, from a man who spent five years in the CMU with Dad. He too, had heard of Dad's passing and knew of me from the many stories Dad would share during his two hours out each day. He shared how Dad never went anywhere without his Bible, this was his comfort and his protection. He noted Dad was always sharing the Word, and would always be writing letters to me, Mike and our children. He spoke of Dad's loyalty and that you could never trust someone in prison, except for Dad. He was trustworthy, and because of this he respected Dad.

Monday, April 19, 2021, I arrived at *Hope City* to Pastor Q and Angie, and some other church staff. Dad had not yet arrived. It wasn't long before the hearse arrived at the front door. I did not have casket bearers, and my family and friends jumped in to help bring my dad in the doors of a place that meant so much to both of us. Pastor Q, Ben, Red, and Ben's father, BJ, joined together to carry Dad in. This brought my heart joy in the sorrow.

Approximately forty people came that day. Family, friends of mine, and friends of my brother. Dad's sisters, my mom, and uncle. Even friends of Dad's from before he went off on another life journey. The funeral was also live streamed for those who could not attend, which was attended by over twenty others.

In the background on the large screen, hundreds of pictures flipped one by one. Many hugs and many tears as people were able to see Dad for the first time in so many years.

The funeral began, and Pastor Q shared different stories of Dad's faithfulness. It was so good, and so *on point*, I felt compelled to share the transcript:

Kindness, compassion. His memory has a profound impact on many, a man who was marked by what we would describe as three great loves. First, his love for his God. Second, his love for his family. How do we know that? Did Russ make some mistakes? Well, I know he loved his family despite those mistakes, not because I read his letters, but because I loved my family despite my mistakes. One of the things we have to grapple with is that a few bad chapters does not describe the entirety of a life. It didn't for Russ, and it doesn't for you.

Although I never got a chance to meet Russ face to face, or get to know him intimately and personally, MY life has been impacted, profoundly impacted, my world has been turned upside down through the life of Russell Dean Landers, cowboy. My life has been changed. How has it changed? Because Russell in the late 80s led this beautiful brown-haired, brown-eyed girl, who happened to be his neighbor, named Angela to the Lord. It was that initial relationship with Jesus that served as a spark in her heart, as I discovered my own spiritual journey with God.

And that's what we learn about life, in particular about Russ. That our lives are limited. There is a certain amount of time that we have all been given to breathe in and breathe out and a day will come when we exhale our last breath...and although our lives are limited, our legacy and our impact in the lives of the people around us, they can be limitless. I never met him with these brown eyes, but I am grateful for that brown-eyed girl who he loved on at a young age and led her to Jesus, and now her life and my life have been greatly enriched for these past twenty-seven years.

Never, Never, write off a book based on the chapter you are currently reading. My past only tells you where I've been, it has nothing to do with where I am going. If you can do that, then not only will you be free from the shame of your own faults, but you can celebrate the life of someone else who doesn't measure up to your standards. And this is why we are celebrating the life of a great man, who did great good in spite of where he was.

As we were talking, preparing for today, Amy's got this box she's been carrying around, it's like a security blanket. It's got a ton of letters, pictures and I mean everywhere she goes she's carrying it around. As we were thumbing through it and stories and how they were able to spend time with Russ, that alone was a miracle. Right before he took his last breath, I said, 'I can't help but think as I hear you talk about your dad, I think about this person in the Bible who changed the legacy of the world. This man has impacted the lives of billions of billions of people. Your life has been impacted by this man. If you live in America, America was built on Judeo Christian ethics and principles, which means the life of this man helped build a nation. I mean your dad reminds me of this man, and you're like, who is he? I mean whenever I think of your dad I think of this guy. He's got a little bit of a track record. They go "who is he?" This guy—he was a prisoner. He was in prison for murder. His name was Paul. Have you ever heard of him? This man was named Paul.

What impacted me is that she had a box full of letters, and then I realized, people started emailing our church, comments like, "Hey we want you to know Russ meant the world to us." And then these Facebook messages started coming in from all the people that Russ was writing, and I went, OH MY GOSH…do you realize that over 50% of the New Testament is letters written by Paul while he sat in prison? Let that sink in for a second.

It's not where you are that determines your contributions to the world. My goodness if being in prison prevents someone from fulfilling their purpose then we'd never have the Bible. He didn't do his time. He invested his time in what mattered most. His three passions. His God, his family and his country.

When I think of your dad, I think of a man who was a GIANT for the kingdom, who inspired, impacted and pushed people forward who loved well and lived a remarkable life. He was authentic, he lived his purpose, he was enthusiastic, he was servant hearted. You heard from prison guards how he impacted the context of the prison that he was in. Do you know what it takes to smile in a dungeon? Do you know what it takes to be positive when you know where you will lay your head the rest of your life? Do you know what it takes to hold out hope when you know others have written you off? The kind of strength and endurance in the midst of adversity and ridicule and scorn of others? To choose to smile and not speak evil? But choose love? Do you know what kind of strength your father possessed?

So, when you tell his story, you tell them that. You tell them of his nature and his character, that although he was a man who fought, he chose love, he chose service, he chose humility. Tell them of a man who made a difference with the life that he lived. If you do that—you will honor your father.

The service, with music that Dad loved played in the background as memories were shared.

Mike shared the journey of three chapters. First chapter included Mike as a child and all of the memories he had up to the age of ten. The second chapter, Dad's incarceration. The difficulties of growing up as a young man, with an incarcerated father. And the third chapter, so short, but that visit he had with Dad, and the forgiveness that took place in that hospital room. The circle of life and how it brought them back to each other in the end, there in that hospital room in Terre Haute, Indiana.

I then had my opportunity. I shared the journey of living life with Dad, despite where we were. I shared about a man who left one day and went on a journey that although hurt me and so many others in the beginning, ended up putting himself at God's disposal in the deepest, darkest dungeons in America and led others to Jesus one conversation, one prayer at a time. I shared the depth of his heart, giving examples from phone calls and letters. Sharing stories like his thankfulness for his sink, or bowl, as he described it and the little bottle of shampoo, and how he reminded me to pray for those who may not have those luxuries. I wasn't sure if I would make it through my speech, but I did and was able to say the things I needed to say.

Jessica then wrote a speech and shared her story of redemption, redemption for inmate 05177-046 and how he was so much more than a number. Jessica knew my dad, only faintly from when we were children, but she, along with my closest friends had lived this journey with me for so many years. Her heart poured out on that stage as she honored my father in so many ways

As we closed, and the funeral ended, everyone began to leave. I was given one more moment with Dad, before he left. I stood over him, placed my hand on his hand, and one last time, thanked him. "Daddy, I forgive you for the journey that hurt me. I thank you for the gift of your relationship with Jesus. This was the greatest inheritance you could have ever left for my children and me. I am eternally grateful. I am sorry Daddy for the injustices, and that I couldn't get you out. I fought with everything in me—our team fought. But Dad—you are now home, you are now in eternal glory, and I will see you again."

The same friends and family then carried Dad out to the waiting hearse. I walked behind them and watched as Dad was placed inside.

I would have Dad cremated so he could spend the rest of my earthly life at home, with me. Letters, emails and Facebook messages continued. There was some comfort in knowing of all the people who were impacted by Dad's love and his story of resilience.

A week later, Dad was home. He was placed in a gift from one of my dearest friends, Sarah, who gave me a handmade wooden box with a cross on the front.

Now I wait for his things as I knew the challenges, the hurt, the sadness this would bring. Little did I know the impact receiving Dad's things would have on my life, and the vision of my destiny.

A week went by, and I began to find myself with a newfound peace that I hadn't experienced in so many years. There was peace knowing that Dad was no longer in twenty-two or twenty-four hour lock down, there was peace in knowing there was no more sadness, no more hurt for him. The many years of prison took a toll on him, a toll that he so carefully protected me from. I found it difficult to describe this peace to anyone, I still longed for another phone call or another letter, but there was a new feeling now. Dad was dancing with Jesus, he was with his Creator, his first love, and I could find a small amount of comfort in this.

On a Wednesday afternoon my doorbell rang, and there on my steps were two large boxes. I knew what they were, I knew

this was my daddy's belongings. I carried the boxes in and sat them on my living room floor. There was some hesitancy in opening them, as I knew how difficult diving into this unseen world would be.

Opening the first box, I began to pull out gray sweatshirts, as I put them to my nose in an attempt to smell Dad. Then t-shirts, two of them, both gray along with two pairs of shorts, underwear and sweatpants. His gray stocking hat, socks, three pairs. His shoes, the old-style Reebok. Over the counter medications, lots of them. Halls cough drops, several other cough suppressants. This reminded me of Dad's cough that started back in January. Although I would hear it over the phone, I had no idea how bad it really was, considering he was living with metastasized lung

cancer. Generic pain relievers, skin creams. His cup, a large clear cup with a black straw. His padlock, toothbrush and toothpaste along with other hygiene items. I had some comfort in knowing he was the last to touch these items for the most part. I picked up and held each and every item. His watch. He loved this watch; he wore it every day. Then, his Bible, three Bibles to be exact. It was well used, noted with color pencil highlights, comments, quotes written throughout, a twin to his Bible he left at home so many years ago.

The second box, on the top, contained his little radio. This radio and headphones gave Dad a lifeline to the outside world. He would listen to his alma mater, *The University of Northern Iowa* sports games on this radio, along with talk shows and listen to *oldies but goodies*. Countless manila envelopes contained paperwork. The calendars: Dad would draw monthly calendars, using colored pencils and he would keep one for himself and send them out to Mike, Mom, and I, each and every month. An envelope with the stamp sheets, although there were no stamps, I saw how he would tear the "sticker border" off and use it as tape. How creative Dad was. A folder with perfectly cut out pictures, pictures of landscapes, tractors, fishing poles and other things that Dad loved so very much which he would attach to our letters. Spiritual tracts, stories from the Bible that someone must have given to him, and he would give out to others. A list of each and every letter that went out to myself, my brother, my mom, and every letter that was delivered to him, with the date and time he sent them. So detailed, so much time to do these things that brought him joy. An envelope of all of his notes on the days and times he had served.

A piece of paper, two to be exact captured my attention. Dad wrote on a piece of paper sideways, "5'10 ½ 185 pds" very large across the paper. The other, "05177046 95328175…" Dad's inmate number and his attorney's phone number. I am assuming this was from the hole, where dad had been taken when he was sick, the one he described with the dirt floor, the cell he thought he was going to die in. Alone. He must have held these papers up in the window for his friend to contact his attorney.

There were a couple of pages of Dad's attempt to write a letter once he began to have difficulty seeing. His writing quickly became nearly illegible. His beautiful handwriting, now running down the page.

Several books, a couple of photo albums which as I looked through made my heart smile, all of the pictures he still had that I had sent over the years. He cherished this book. Even some pictures of friends he met along his journey.

Then, a piece of paper stood out like a diamond sparkling in the water. It was folded the long way and numbered 502 to 632 in

1000 GIFTS FROM A 7 X 10

one column down one side, with writing after each number and then on the other 633-769 on the other side. The first note written on one line was "the ants building their home."

I continued to read, and then continued digging. I found a page nearly identical to the first, lists starting with number 1. And there was the title. "1000 Gifts."

Dear God.

His list of 1000 things he was thankful for—thankful for this list from his cell where he spent days, nights, months and years. HE WAS THANKFUL FOR THE ANTS BUILDING THEIR HOME!

How could I ever, ever know the depth of his heart, the depth of his love for life, his humble heart? His ability to recognize the little things he did have and his gratefulness for the people in his life. How does one see the beauty in life from a 7x10 cell? How could anyone come up with this list in the conditions Dad was in? My tears would not stop. The tears flooded my face, flooded my heart, all the way to my core.

My son Alex, in his infinite wisdom took the papers and read over the list and it was in this moment he said to me, "Mom, this is it. This is the title of your book. You have to tell Grandpa's story." My greatest pain had unlocked my greatest purpose.

I must tell this story.

I must tell this story.

"One Thousand Gifts" Ann Voskamp Ontario, Canada
2008 Echareisteo - Fight for Joy! Thanksgiving! (Might rase the dead)
Gratitude Journal - List all the gifts God gives us.

The 1000 gifts showed faith and courage, despite isolation and despair. This list proved Dad's full belief in God. *Did he know the treasure he was leaving me with?*

The first entry #1: Breath. #2: Strength. #3: Love. #4: The written Word. #5: Conversation with Amy by phone call.

As you continue to read through the list, the basic things, the simplest of things. #16: Needs met. #21: Warm, clean clothing. #24: My prayer room always open. #32: Jesus calling — 8th of Feb. #33: in the light. #36: Philippians 4:13.

#42: Still waters speak.

#51: Clean warm shower.

#58: Smiles exchanged.

#65: Silence is golden.

#67: Almond bar — Yummmm!

#68: Jesus is with me.

#80: quiet.

#86: Good phone convo. With Mike (Friday 7pm)

#96: My heart often moved.

#98: Things to laugh about.

#105: Time.

#107: Safe in the Word.

#110: Fresh air.

#118: Sharp colored pencils.

#174: Remembering...

#183: Bobby moved to a better place...

#193: I see the ants industry

#502: Hot water received for coffee

#511: Clean floor.

Although dad never reached the 1000th gift, he ended on number #769: Family and friends planning for picking me up!

Gut wrenching sadness. He was waiting. He believed until the end that he would be coming home. His hope never wavered. His faith never wavered.

As I continued to read through all of the things my dad was grateful for, I began to learn more about who my dad was, who he was within the walls of the prison. Dad's hope for his future which was rooted in heaven spoke from the black ink on the pages. The depth of his thankfulness of things that we overlook each and every day. I knew Dad, I knew him better than anyone, but this list taught me more about the character of the man I was blessed to call Dad. The thoughts of when I felt my life was a struggle, when I was feeling sad or depressed, how dare I? The reality of the things that mattered most in life hit me the hardest at this moment.

I now understand the value of the small things: laughter, relaxing, SILENCE, freedom, music, a cup of coffee. The joy of the presence of the Lord. How often we forget.

A phone call, and #550: my little fan sings on. We forget the promises made, promises from our Father, to meet all our needs, but Dad didn't forget this. The fact that he could acknowledge *the little fan singing* within a cell that reached up to 115 degrees in the summer.

The Apostle Paul wrote a letter of gratitude, from the inside of prison walls to the Philippians. Philippians 4:12: *I know what it is to be in need, and I know what it is to have plenty. I have learned the secret of being content in any and every situation.*

There is value to being content. In a book I read years ago, I recall reading about Corrie ten Boom, who wrote of her gratefulness for the flea infestation within her barracks of the concentration camp she was in during World War II. She was thankful for the fleas because they kept the guards away. She used this time to share Bible stories with others.

I learned through this list the value of gratitude, even in the worst of situations. Paul's example, Corrie ten Boom's examples, and *1000 Gifts* make me reveal a depth of gratitude for my life in a new light. A light that is no longer shallow to the realities of the world.

Dad did not feel sorry for himself. He used this time, these moments in silence to reveal the gift in what "was." He valued the small things. Found light in the darkness.

Today, because of the *1000 Gifts* left behind, I choose to be intentional in the small things. To always, always look for the good. I choose to find gratitude, no matter where I am. To look for love when others live in gloom and despair. I choose to live a more fulfilling, joyful life in order to be a direct reflection of the *1000 Gifts* and Jesus, even through the storms. I choose to listen to that "still small voice" that whispers so gently in my ear during life's chaos. Throughout my life, in the mistakes I make, I remember I am forgiven, and remember to be thankful for another chance. In the storm, the turbulent waters, I was made brave, this too must be identified, and noted in my heart. Even in the midst of overwhelming, unforeseen situations, I search, seek and discover the goodness, the gift the situation may bring. By seeing the good, in the storms, I can learn to be above any circumstance and refocus my attention to what matters.

On the days where the sunshine beams and the birds sing, I choose to be thankful. I choose to identify the happiness, and not just brush it aside. I choose to live because of the impact of the *1000 Gifts*. My gratitude, understanding and compassion, grace and mercy, kindness and forgiveness, all strengthened.

I am braver.

CHAPTER 12

Faith Remains

The events that began to transpire over twenty-eight years ago as of this writing, have been my experiences for over half my life, developing me into the strong woman I have become today. Reflecting back on so many circumstances that could have gone one way or the other, good or bad, I conclude and stand firm in the fact that God is in control. Events that made me who I am today. Circumstances that opened my eyes to a world that I may have never known, were it not for the choice to go down the path my dad chose back in 1993.

When I think of Dad, and his story, and all of the significance his journey had on myself and countless others, I am reminded of Jesus's marvelous mercy. I am reminded that "all sins people do can be forgiven" and for the hurt Dad caused myself and others, I believe he was forgiven. My journey of forgiving Dad began as soon as he left and blossomed into the unique relationship that it became. Dad was my best friend. He listened with intent, guided me throughout my life for nearly twenty-four years, from a prison, and sometimes from one of the darkest units in America. He showed me grace, prayed for me and my children and loved me through paper and phone calls. Dad was my hero. My hero, for standing firm in his faith throughout all the days, months and years away, he truly was my hero.

I too, spent twenty-four years, eight months and one day in prison, without ever committing a crime. I learned how to navigate the unique challenges that come with having an incarcerated loved one. I learned to love from afar, to have great patience in times in my life where I "just wanted my dad" and how to have a dad who was alive, that I could not touch, except through glass. I learned how to walk through difficult seasons of life, and good seasons in life with one focus—God. Dad lived this. He spoke this daily. He slept in comfort having endless faith in God despite his circumstances. I learned how Dad's steadfast faith impacted a culture, which all too often was a dark, dirty, sometimes violent place. I learned to have grace for those who were in Dad's situation and began to focus on how we can "just do better."

When I look back to Dad's standoff, the sentencing process, the events that took place in New York, my experience in Rikers Island, meeting and having the opportunity to pray with some beautiful souls, watching events transpire over national news, prison phone calls, the unknown when the phone calls didn't come, the visits and having to walk away and leave Dad, the "behind the glass" visits, Dad's tears over the phone sharing he can now "see the sky" after 11 years.

I learned to have a faith that surpasses all understanding. Dad taught me this.

No matter your circumstances, it is a mindset. It is an intentional act to wake up in the morning, breathe in the air, and be thankful for where you are—no matter where you are.

Miller: *"It is sufficient to trust the living God, and not worry about earthly things, for the beginning of worry is the end of faith and the beginning of faith is the end of worry."* This was a quote in a letter from dad in 2020.

I would like to challenge you, dear reader, to a task that may seem simple, or may seem very difficult, depending on your mindset. Can you write a list of a thousand things YOU are thankful for? Can you write just fifty things you are thankful for, ten, just two?

Can you find happiness no matter where you are? Can you dig deep and begin to see the world from a different perspective? All you need is a sheet of paper and a pen. Inspire yourself by ALL of the things you have in your life that you may have simply looked over each and every day. Let your mind intentionally wander to those things that you often take for granted in the course of your everyday life. What do you see? What do feel? What do you hear?

And while you begin the journey of a new thankfulness in your heart, the question remains. How do we "just do better?" What does this look like, where do we begin when it comes to those incarcerated, from the sentencing phase all the way through the life of the incarcerated individual? How do we ensure, the over sentencing and punishment doesn't outweigh the crime? How do we ensure families have some peace, a voice, a role in the process?

My thoughts begin with a movement in the direction of creating a "Justice that Restores." What does this look like?

The definition of retribution, let's start here. Retribution: to give what is due either as a reward or a punishment. It can also be described as an "eye-for-an-eye" or proportional approach to the criminal justice system. Retribution recognizes that each and every person has value and potential, which doesn't change because someone commits a crime and is sentenced to prison. EVERY person has value. EVERY person has potential. If we set a goal, as a system to seek retribution, we then seek to only punish the wrongdoing, in a way that is proportional to the crime committed and does not diminish a person's value as a human being. This proportional response signifies the human value of any victims as well. A system focused on retribution says that a person must be punished for their crime, however not punished more than they deserve.

Dad was warehoused, not restored. There must remain a value of the human being because they are, they live, breathe and more likely than not have a yearning to do better when released. Those that do not and remain a danger must be held, however, held in a place that values their humanity.

I think of the sentencing process as a puzzle. There are several pieces to the puzzle when someone is sentenced. The crime itself, the victim impact, the sentencing guidelines, and the threat to the community are all pieces that fit into the puzzle. Knowing the impact of incarceration in America, it is critical to evaluate the various stages and issues associated with sentencing and punishment. When I reflect on Dad's sentencing and the excessive amount of time given to him, it was unjust, cruel and even on some levels irrational.

I think of the opportunities missed early on. Excessive punishment violates human dignity to the incarcerated individual, as well as those closest to them. If only the judge would have had the small piece to this puzzle, and considered the impact on a daughter, the loss of Dad in my life and how this would affect me for the rest of my life. Dad had someone who cared, someone who loved him, and a "life sentence" was far beyond justice. The missed opportunity for restoration was shameful.

Creating a system and following through with the design, starting with the hiring of employees working with the incarcerated. A mission of each and every system is as simple as valuing human life, a mission of believing people can change. Those hired must have the qualities of respect, empathy and dignity each and every day at work, always remembering these are somebody's loved ones, despite what they have done on their worst days. These are someone's daddy, mothers, sisters, brothers... someone's sons, someone's daughters. This job is not easy and takes a toll on staff. The sadness, anger and frustrations that come with a job in such a system, requires a servant's heart on so many levels.

Prison oversight in all institutions, no matter State or Federal. Having an outside agency review everything from sentencing to medical care of the incarcerated, to discipline and the overall culture of our institutions can have tremendous impacts on cultures that are broken, resulting in hurt, frustration and behaviors within the walls that could have been avoided. There is value to treating people like people, there truly is. I think of those named, that day in the visiting room in 2019, those he pointed out, "she is nice to me," "he truly cares." Those words were a sunlight to my heart, a true comfort that "they" were nice to him.

My thoughts should not be misunderstood. I believe there should be consequences to criminal behavior. There are certainly people who must be in prison, for community safety. Absolutely. However, for those, like Dad, who was at the end of life, who had spent years behind bars, years in a cell, there was almost an act of revenge instead of justice. The harsh sentence given to him left us both to pay a costly price. I believe there should be changes made to ensure our system is more sensible, where victims and communities are safer, yet people are not disproportionately punished.

Take the shackles off a man unable to see, unable to walk, unable to wake up. Take the shackle off. Human dignity should always prevail.

There are so many other daughters out there. It has become part of the American lifestyle to have a family member or loved one in prison. The numbers are astonishing, impacting more than people know. Do you have a loved one, a family member, a friend or are YOU incarcerated?

Our country continues to lead the world in incarceration. The last numbers I could find reveal in 2020, one year prior to Dad's death more than five million people were under correctional supervision in some capacity and almost two million people were in prison or jail.

My own thoughts – we continue to "challenge the process" This was something I learned early in my career, a way of leadership that I understood and made sense. While we continue to maintain safety and security for our communities, we begin to look at the person first. Outdated policy or policy and practice that counter the impact of "tough on crime" rhetoric only reinforces incarceration. Let's start here. Discussions of "what can be." What can our system look like to ensure restorative justice? Maximum sentences with annual reviews/consideration for those who have made progress? There are so many missed opportunities to ensure families and those who commit a crime are not given life sentences for "what one thinks they could do."

We must "just do better" and my hope for this book, for Dad's *1000 Gifts*, is that we all take a few moments and begin to collaborate within our states, within our communities, read and become knowledgeable in what our system could look like, where a man, like my father, doesn't have to spend years in a cell day after day, without coming out, doesn't have to live with unbearable pain from sores all over his body for years, a daughter can visit her dad and give him a hug, or doesn't have to die, alone, when he meets all of the requirements to be released.

A judge who accepts motions daily for three weeks should not recuse themselves the day to decide a case where the inmate is unable to walk, see or even wake up. The situations like these, that leave scars and wounds to the soul of loved ones should not be acceptable.

Awareness brings steps to take swift action. Take the time to learn how our system works, and how we can "just do better." Remembering the value of all human beings, being intentional about connecting with groups throughout our country that are slowly, but surely having an impact to inspire change. I think of FAMM and all that they did to help me and Dad in our unique circumstance.

You have a voice; I have a voice. There can and will be impacts and an awakening when we all begin to focus on "just do better" and seek grace, mercy and justice, remembering all people are created in God's image, and no life is beyond HIS reach.

Dad is home, eternally, and his ashes are home with me. His shackles are removed. I think about him every single day. I think of the thousand gifts, I talk to others about him and his story. I find solace and comfort when I share. I reflect on the thousands of phone calls and reread letters that are a catalyst to continue to live out the values I learned over so many years of walking through this life with Dad.

While not perfect by any means, he was my dad, and through it all, gave me a depth of understanding that will impact my children, and hopefully so many others walking on a journey similar to ours.

We have to "just do better."

1000 GIFTS FROM A 7 X 10

CHAPTER THIRTEEN

Landers Family Photos, Letters, Mementos

Early years with Dad and his new Mustang. Amy, Ryan & Dad.

Dad hanging ornaments on the tree when I was too little to reach the top of the tree - 1980.

Dad and Mike posing while putting up the Christmas tree.

LANDERS FAMILY PHOTOS, LETTERS, MEMENTOS

June 24, 2003 – Ben was 14 days old here, his first and last time ever physically touching Grandpa. Alex, Amy, and Dad – El Reno Federal Prison.

Amy around the age of six, holding one of my prize fish. This was taken on my grandfather's farm in Greene, Iowa, roughly 1983.

Ryan Landers, my brother. June 14, 1974 – January 7, 2000

Me and my daddy.

Amy, Alex, and Dad – El Reno Federal Prison, 2001

Dad's first prison picture – El Reno, roughly 1999.

Dad

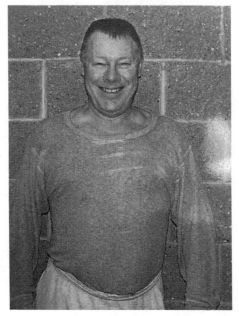

CMU Unit - always smiling.

Pastor Q speaking at Dad's funeral.

Amy, Alex, and Ben

1000 GIFTS FROM A 7 X 10

A702
P1

by: "The Light" 5 May 2020, Tuesday
Get a FREE Emergency radio w/batteries
needed for. [gettheradio.com]

dear Amy,

The Lord ever present is there even now, as He is here. There is a chill in the air here, as I write. I'm going to put my sweat shirt on. Lots of writing and keyboarding as I make up for no copier. The financial grip is ahead of those, as well. A fellow traveler was told when he ask about the copies, "It's not in the budget." Absurd! We pay 15¢ per copy. It is a ridiculous profit center and they can't keep it going?

Coast to Coast AM's guest last night is not at all confident about the economy. The usury money scheme is careening out of control. Paying people to NOT produce DOES NOT put bread on the table!

I know I may be speaking out and not being heard, but it would be very wise to be gardening this season. Not as an extra, as a stop gap against very real hunger. The practical reality is not unlike 1929. Our grand parents lived out of the garden and on the livestock, chickens, eggs, milk they raised. There was no alternative. Prayer and thanksgiving. It is the Lord who provides. The garden spot is a crucial gift from Him. Before I graduated from high school we bought little from grocers or McDonalds. It was all from our own garden and livestock. Have we all forgotten something??? Food must be raised. It does not just majically appear. The Word is clear, "Those who will not work, will not eat."

Who will see "The Light"?
Prayerfully consider.

6631 Wedgewood
Mail box
garage
Garden Space
house deck
Lilac

Dad's letters, so brilliantly and creatively written,
each and every letter for over 24 years.

Cowboy drawing – this was Dad's other "thumb print."
The little cowboy was often found throughout Dad's letters.

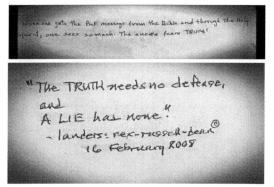

Notes of encouragement Dad made while in prison.

Dad's watch he loved so much, along with his favorite Bible. He had six Bibles in his belongings, this was his favorite.

1000 GIFTS FROM A 7 X 10

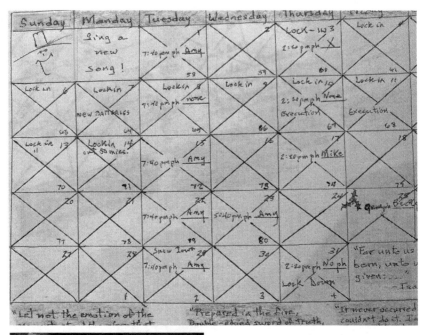

The calendars Dad would hand draw for others and mail out monthly. He would note birthdays and other significant events here. Every month. Every family member received one.

Dad's prison badge. Inmate 05177-046

lle, remember my purpose in life first written in 1989.

> My purpose in life is to be an enthusiastic, positive servant of YHVH Messiah, Jesus, the Christ, strong and firm in the WORD, The TRUTH and every day of my life claiming life, liberty and happiness for me and my fellow workers in the Kingdom of YHVH and so I am.
> Thanks be to YHVH
> I am a cowboy.
>
> Rex - Russell - dean Von der Haus Von landers

Dad's purpose in life.

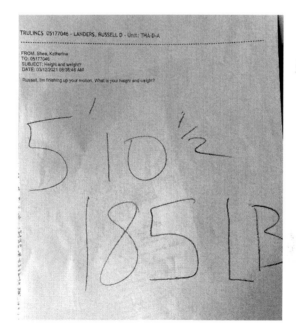

Dad's response to Kat.

1000 GIFTS FROM A 7 X 10

1000 gifts

1 - breath
2 - strength
3 - love
4 - Written Word
5 - Conversation with Amy by ph call
6 - Grace re cell
7 - Feel the strength
8 - e-mail with Pat Shannon
9 - Clean move for room next door
10 - Feeling is mixed
11 - Danny, Alex's safe return
12 - Music — warms
13 - Friends share
14 - Financial gifts bless
15 - Forces for liberty moving steadily
16 - Needs met
17 - Christ's love now
18 - Blessings never ending
19 - Help for us all
20 - Certain hope for liberty soon
21 - Warm — clean clothing
22 - Cloved once well
23 - Chocolate ice-cream
24 - My prayer room ever open
25 - Hot coffee, breakfast
26 - comfort — cleanliness
27 - Insight — wisdom
28 - Direction
29 - healing
30 - Inspiring materials
31 - Oatmeal — service
32 - Jesus calling — Book
33 - to the flight
34 - Friends at breakfast
35 - Blessed
36 - Philippians 4:13
37 - God's glory present
38 - Friend and I reflect on psychopaths
39 - silence — spirit present
40 - Snow — fall — beauty
41 - Cats are pleased it appears
42 - Still Waters speak
43 - Chill in the air
44 - Chat/Bagel w/ friend Mario
45 - Psalm 92

46 - Word for liberty in the air
47 - Blessed Bible study
48 - Hand full of salted peanuts
49 - We have new World Book here
50 - Quiet Time — Thinking time
51 - Clean — warm shower
52 - The WORD here for me
53 - Letters needed for friends
54 - Guidance for living
55 - Bagel w/ Mario — conversation
56 - Devotions w/ Jesus
57 - Coffee is warm
58 - Smiles exchanged
59 - letter off to Marty Bea
60 - Courage of the Lord, the Word, Jn 1:1
61 - Geranegaret — garden of riches
62 - No complaints — No murmuring
63 - Friends arising
64 - The suffer-8 heals by hand of The Lord
65 - Silence is golden
66 - SLIGHT EDGE touching me
67 - Almond Bar — Umm mm!
68 - Jesus is with me
69 - Ooh! I love chocolate ice-cream
70 - Ava's letter blessed me
71 - A gift for my German language
72 - Child's in our heart
73 - The Lord Jesus is my Redeemer
74 - Umm — Almond bar
75 - A German language book gift
76 - Helpful meal
77 - Letter sent off for Mike/
78 - good fitness, aim
79 - nap refreshed me
80 - quiet
81 - AUTA BUY came
82 - A new movie
83 - Study with Curt — Samuel — Hope
84 - blessings — cereal breakfast
85 - Chick Pok's — contact
86 - Good ph. conv'n with Mike (Tues by 7pm)
87 - Almond bar w/ coffee
88 - Close with The Holy Spirit
89 - Humility, w/ honor
90 - Gandhi speaks from the dust
91 - I am a flee man
92 - silence often to be treasured
93 - Jesus walked me through letter for W
94 - BBQ chicken sandwich
95 - A movie sat in Chicago
96 - My heart often needed

LANDERS FAMILY PHOTOS, LETTERS, MEMENTOS

570 - peanuts and almonds
571 - David has a good motion 3584(a) stacking
572 - sheep to be separate - satan being exposed.
573 - Christian Rock Catalogue in
574 - Good conversation with Amy
575 - Glad for Amy and her family - new home
576 - Penny back with her people
577 - The Lord sending help with Amy for Arleae, Keoki, Dana Voss - Need The WORD
578 - Quiet, peaceful
579 - Word of thanks from Kat Shea
580 - Book: History of SS/training
581 - Written WORD speaks
582 - Idolatry of corporate tyranny EXPOSED!
583 - JESUS, The Rock, our strong foundation
584 - Awake, blessed, well rested
585 - Labels approved Amy, Ted Elden
586 - Jan Markel - Michelle Bachmann
587 - Quiet Monday morning
588 - Pastor Jeffress powerful message for Christ's foundation for USA.
589 - I'm reminded of the patriarchal order.
590 - Thinking of Craig & Meryl's Bohlen
591 - Lessons for our Adoot-Israel people.
592 - Direction from above
593 - Good conversation with Becky
594 - Word of Stella Jean - wonderful.
595 - Word of Andrew and Allison
596 - email out for Amy
597 - Steven Quayle on Coast-to-Coast
598 - Clothes for Marty B
599 - Good lesson on Demons by Dr. Robert Jeffress
600 - letter for Truman Knutson
601 - Reminded of One Thousand Gifts - Ann VosKamp
602 - Rec'd: Like Clay Under the Seal, Pastor Dean Odle
603 - Rec'd: BANANA MAN by Ray Comfort (BLESSED)
604 - My legs strengthened
605 - A quiet morning (Sun 19 Juli 2021)
606 - Thankful for devotions
607 - Thank you Lord for showing flat earth.
608 - AFP providing valuable insights
609 - Great call w/ Amy; 28 Juli, Donna tag
610 - Commissary blessing
611 - Readied Becky's & Katherine's B-Day cards
612 - Timothy gave me a drink treat
613 - Timothy, I and Ron Hansen prayed
614 - The Lord is opening gates - enemies flee
615 - The rats are jumping ship
616 - The name Jesus Christ is prevailing.
617 - LOVE as JChrist 1st loved us. Mt 5:38-48
618 - Good for sharing
619 - Thank the Lord He saw me through this mourning.
620 - Jesus speaks to me.
621 - Choc. chip cookies and coffee ☕
622 - American Free Press
623 - YHVH Messiah present, guides me.
624 - Two calls 2d & 3d Sept - Amy
625 - labels approved, more updated
626 - Tim and Wendy shared burritos
627 - Rec'd Graham crackers
628 - Visit with Dennis Nixon
629 - Visits with David Hankson
630 - Visits Marie and Don
631 - Dennis shared treat w/ me
632 - Visit, prayer meet Timothy

502 - Hot water rec'l for coffee. '17 Mei
503 - Good conversation with Dave Hinkson
504 - Copied calendar & Dana to I
505 - Supper beef stroganoff - good (18 Mei)
506 - Medical records sent out 32 Mei - Frietag
507 - Conversation with Becky
508 - Michael's 38th birthday
509 - The Lord ever-present
510 - The Lord speaks, his angels speak
511 - Clean floor
512 - Chicken dinner
513 - Radio - Rush - NPR
514 - Studium Race and the Bible
515 - Good visit with Timothy Fitzpatrick
516 - Presence with The Lord.
517 - Whole TRUTH.
518 - Marty - angelic letter in
519 -
520 - Prayers answered - Thank YHVH messiah
521 - A day The Lord has made
522 - Giving thanks to The Lord Jesus
523 - Peanuts and Almonds ✓
524 - Fruit of the Spirit
525 - a banana
526 - Sweet treat from Robert - w/ coffee ☕
527 - Choc. covered peanuts from David
528 - Conversations - fellow travelers (30 Mei)
529 - Evening chicken dinner
530 - Lord's Keeping today cool
531 - Lord spoke while I prepared and slept.
532 - New Muscle Machines - funlook
533 - Almond nut bar treat
534 - Peaceful, refreshing reign
535 - Seeing The WORD in all.
536 - Messed by Ravi Zacharia
537 - Commissary day
538 - Beautiful symphonic pc we played 554 cargo
539 - My little fan Keeps comforting
540 - My order for next week ready
541 - Jehette Medford blessing to Keith
542 - Great Duke Ellington on NPR
543 - Lord's healing all
544 - Economy bouncing back...
545 - Jazz on NPR...
546 - Devotional tea
547 - Out 3 hrs - PT - 9 June, Decorating
548 - Sorted and stored letters
549 - Rain painting the window
550 - My little fan sings on and on
551 - Strength in The Lord
552 - Friend came by earlier - Hello DR+ ☺
553 - Apple sparkling taste ☺
554 - Heinrich Himmler photo biography
555 - SAINTS history 1846 —
556 - Hurricane rain from Gulf of America
557 - Thanksgiving reminder
558 - Quiet & cool - peace
559 - All is healing by his stripes
560 - Reminders of His victory - Quiet
561 - Flag blowing shows weather
562 - A wife nag
563 - The Lord hears and answers my prayers
564 - Jesus life manifest in us.
565 - Some chocolate covered peanuts.
566 - Workman's claim copied
567 - Dr. Samuel Kennedy Teacher Birthright
568 - Proverbs 23
569 - The Lord Jesus present

Scott Gottlieb — on Fox

175

1000 GIFTS FROM A 7 X 10

633 - Quiet and cool - nice
634 - Sharing with sis Carol Asher
635 - Cool day
636 - Prayer and eucharisteo with Timothy
637 - 2d Chronicles 7:14 revealed to me
628 - The new day fresh and inviting
629 - Special lunch, ice-cream cone
630 - Every spot head to toe, inside-out healing
631 - Jesus guiding, teaching, keeping me!
632 - Got a hair cut
633 - Blessed with phone call to Amy - late in 9/1/2020
634 - letter out for Ben
635 - letter out for Ava
636 - Ireneaus Knutson's letter arrived
637 - letter from Our Daily Bread
638 - Wonderful call w/ Amy & Penny
639 - Hot water for coffee
640 - Prayer, The written word, devotions, quiet
641 - BOT radio on-air
642 - Conversation w/ Mike
643 - Letter to Cat, Jiovanni
644 - 3 small cakes, cereal, coffee
645 - The Burner Review
646 - Quiet time with Jesus, The WORD
647 - Inspiration
648 - Commissary
649 - Stephen Shirley Jr - Jesus...10/22 came in
700 - Letter at Monty Bar blessings
701 - Cell, e-mails, phone with family
702 - Quiet devotions
703 - Toward Mother, ideal health in Jesus
704 - Liberty swim 23 Oct 2020
705 - Glory - Trust in Jesus

706 - The earth FLAT, Heaven above — TRUTHS
707 - Coffee is HOT, just right
708 - Blessings in the WORD
709 - Amy Coney Barrett to US Sup. Ct
710 - Commissary came Wed. 28 Oct.
711 - Spoke w/ Amy (28 Oct)
712 - Psalm 91 Study, prayer w/ Timothy
713 - Chocolate Pop Tarts and coffee
714 - strawberry pop tart - Apple - peanuts
715 - lovinforhiddall.com
716 - I am directly Christ's - men pleasure NO!
717 - Well rested, coffee/tarts up, time w/ the Lord
718 - Time keeps flying
719 - Good conversation with friend Don
720 - Wow! Cinnamon roll
721 - Blessing in devotions
722 - Coffee, oat meal and Tarts.
723 - Inspiration for sharing
724 - Peggy's right - No notification
725 - Jesus has heard our prayers, results are the
726 - Good rest
727 - Devotions - blessings
728 - Coffee, chip cookies, Tarts
729 - Blessing for sound body, mind, spirit!
730 - Good ph calls w/ Kat 15 of Nov week
731 - Goodph calls w/ Amy 1st of Nov week
732 - Rec'd Dec Antibley
733 - Rec'd Dec Hemmings Motor News
734 - Commissary today - 25 Nov 2020
735 - special Thanksgiving meal
736 - Late: Mark present
737 - Pres. Trump Thanksg. greetings for troops
738 - The Light, Matt. 5:14
739 - Janet McCloud - racing teens (others) 11/27
740 - Penny w/ her people
741 - Also spared serious injury by Jesus.

742 - Understanding the Times 11/28
743 - Travel flight of all
744 - News favoring Pres. Trump, 14 Dec 2020
745 - Blessings
746 - Good talk w/ Amy - concern 4 Arlena
747 - Huge exposure of Fraud election
748 - Rec'd Christmas bag - snacks
749 - Commissary blessings
750 - We're the seed planters - Thank God
751 - Spokes people standing with Jesus
752 - Christmas ph. conversations w/ Becky
753 - Christmas dinner - treats
754 - Devotions and prayers
755 - Scrambled eggs
756 - Warm sun peeks through the window
757 - Prayer after prayer mile + mile
758 - The Clay Under A Seal - Rev. Dean Odle
759 - Special New Year Day meal
760 - Letters this week 1-23
761 - Become God teach
762 - Thankful for cough meds
763 - Wonderful call - Motive for Kim Cat Britt
764 - Amy to call Janice / search out Kim
765 - So glad to get cough drops & liquid
766 - Rest today feeling just fine.
767 - Order for liberty b/4 Wm E Britt
768 - Jesus, The WORD, ever present
769 - Family & friends planning & picking me up!
770 -

CHAPTER 14

Supporting Letters

Note: Following are just a few examples of all the correspondence, documents, etc., over the many years of my daddy's incarceration. There are boxes of medical records, letters, and pleas for help that are too numerous to include.

August 2, 2020

Your Honor,

My name is Amy Landers and I am the daughter of Russell D. Landers who is currently an inmate at Terre Haute Federal Prison in Terre Haute, Indiana.

I want to share a little about myself. I am a 43-year-old single mother of three. My children are Alex who is 24, Ben who is 17 and Ava who is 11. My children have all met their grandfather, but unfortunately it has always been behind glass. He has never physically touched them. I will say he has never missed a birthday for any of them, always sending a card at least a week in advance. I work for the State of Iowa Department of Corrections and have for the last 7 years. Prior to that I was the Executive Director of our county youth shelter and detention facility. I have two brothers, one who is a Principal and Athletic Director of a junior high school and one who has passed.

I want to share some insight of my childhood and my father's role. My dad was just that — my dad who was amazing. He instilled faith in myself and my siblings by planting the seed of Jesus in our hearts, ensuring we were in church on Sunday's and praying before meals. As far back as I can remember my father taught elementary school band for a number of years and then took over my grandfather's insurance company. My dad made birthday's special and would allow me to pick the restaurant and activity of my choice to have a day with just him each and every year. Our favorite place to vacation was Walt Disney World, where we went yearly after contracting fields of corn to detassel to have enough money to go. My dad always worked hard and he instilled that in my siblings and I. My dad and I spent a lot of times fishing as well, and I am very proud to say to this day I take my daughter fishing frequently because of the stillness and peacefulness I found in this activity.

My father grew up on a farm in northwest Iowa in a very small town, Greene, Iowa. This town was one of those farming communities where everyone knows everyone. His parents were farmers and Christian parents who raised my father, the oldest and two younger siblings. I know the work ethic of my father came directly from them as they worked very hard for years to have the nice things they had. They both went to their graves wondering what had happened to their oldest. My father was in band and played football in high-school, continuing his education at the University of Northern Iowa, receiving a Bachelor of Art Degree in Education. My dad married my mother in

1967 and they had three children. He could fix anything: cars, tv's and fishing poles — this is what my mom missed most after my father left and their divorce.

Things began to change with my father when I was approximately 15 years old. At one point my father came home with his license plate upside down on his car, stating he didn't need a license plate because this meant your car belonged to the state. He began having strange thoughts and was befriending people who thought strange things. He felt he and many others were being treated wrong by the government and he was helping to make a change. Due to his strange beliefs, my mother, a 2nd grade teacher immediately put her guard up confronting him on many occasions of his whereabouts and where all these thoughts were coming from. I recall many arguments during this time frame. It was almost as if he was brainwashed at some point. After a few months of this behavior, I remember my mother being afraid, concerned and in disbelief over the new thoughts and strange behaviors of my father. On a warm summer Friday night in August of 1993-1994 my father was planning a two day trip to Minnesota for a meeting. I was scheduled to have a counseling session the following Monday evening and he ensured my mother and I that he would be back to attend this session. He packed a small bag, which couldn't have held more than one outfit and hygiene items and we dropped him off to a man and woman in a parking lot. He said goodbye, and we had no idea he would never return. This after leaving my mother a card with a necklace and ring for their 25th wedding anniversary that same day. After a few days, no phone calls, a missed family counseling appointment and no contact, my mother and grandparents became extremely worried. I remember my mom being on the phone saying things like, "He has been acting so strange, what if he is dead in a ditch somewhere?" My mother went to the local police department here in Waterloo, Iowa and filed a missing person's report. Weeks went by and nothing. I recall worrying and believing my father was dead because he wouldn't do this to me... he wouldn't leave me without saying goodbye. After four weeks, I was at the mall which I did every Friday. I saw a group of people with cowboy clothes, hats & boots on. I thought to myself Dad had been dressing in cowboy clothes, maybe he's in the group, and as I walked closer, there he was. Very clean, cowboy hat, boots and even the big belt buckle. I froze. I watched him briefly until he turned, saw me, and came running to me. I couldn't believe it... he was alive and he is here... at the mall! He hugged me, tears began to flow and he shared that he was undercover for the military and had to leave. I yelled, I asked why... I cried, he cried. I knew by his comment of being undercover he was not ok; something was very wrong. This is not the dad I had known and been so close to my entire 16 years of life. I let him talk and he attempted to introduce me to several people he was with, which I didn't care to meet and wanted him to just come back home. He would never come back home. I ended up having to tell my mother of the encounter that day at the mall — she was devastated, broken and confused by all that had transpired. She immediately filed for divorce. Life changed and my dad was gone.

I spoke with him frequently and the troubles of a young teenage girl became worse after all of this. I ended up running away and living with my father for about six months on the east coast. I witnessed delusional thinking even at such a young and vulnerable age. Something was very wrong and he was not in the same person I had known as my father.

I do not know what happened over the course of that year, I only know he was believing things from so many people that paranoia took over. I know approximately six months after me returning home to my mother, my father ended up in Montana. After doing so many things because of his delusions he found himself in an entirely different reality. A reality that does not exist to you and I — beliefs that were inconceivable to all of us.

My father ended up leaving the standoff in Montana peacefully. There were no victims, peacefully. He would never hurt anyone, and I would state that with 100% certainty. Since his incarceration starting on June 14, 1996, he has been assaulted on numerous occasions, both by staff and other offenders. He has spent over 8 years in 24 hour lock down in a 7x10 cell, with no circulating air. I honestly believe this has contributed to his mental health declining. He is worn, he is tired. I have twice asked for assistance from state representatives, Chuck Grassley and Joni Earnst. Each time they have been extremely helpful. The most recent time his closet associates within the Communications Unit where he is housed, were stabbed, with one of them succumbing to his wounds. ISIS attacked them because they were Christian men. He has lived through horrific isolation, days, hours of no human contact. In twenty-five years over 8 in solitary confinement, and when I go to visit I am behind glass. No human contact. This is horrific treatment. Most recently, since COVID became reality, he has been on 22 hour lock down since the beginning of April. Last August prior to this lockdown I was able to visit him face to face for the first time since he arrived at Terre Haute, over 12 years ago. Thanks to the senators involvement he was moved out of the Communications Unit because his violence propensity level is low and he was moved to the general population. As you can imagine I went for a visit immediately to touch, hug and love on my father. I sat and waited for him to walk in and when he did I could not help but tear up. He was confused and guarded. I hugged him, his first hug in over 12 years, he was brittle. He had sores in his hair, he had sores on his arms. He has complained for years about his skin condition and had no treatment that worked. He says he has Shingles and has been given a cream which does nothing for the pain. When he sat down next to me, my heart broke as he crossed his legs and arms and almost sat in a chair in a fetal position, almost as if to protect himself. His teeth hurt, he's had no dental treatment and three teeth have broken off. I am beside myself with the treatment of my father. 25 years of this. Earlier in the year he was moved back to the CMU unit, with ISIS, lockdown a majority of the time in his 7 x 10 cell. Dangerous when he is out, despite no discipline on his progress report. No answers. He has extreme issues with allergies, always has. Oftentimes he can't catch his breath. He is 70 years old, almost 71. I am scared. Not only because of COVID but because of his age and his fragile body, his fragile mental health.

I received his progress report from the prison a couple months back. The information on the report was not accurate as they have his age, date of birth, education level wrong. This was very concerning. No discipline reports. Numerous classes taken, even GED classes, despite having a BA plus 45. He leads a Christian group. Medical shows little, he is known to pass out from extreme heat in his housing unit.

Your honor, I will allow my father to live with me. I live in Waterloo, Iowa where I am a respected member of this community. My home is safe and in the country. I have a large support group. I helped plant the fastest growing church in Iowa's history, directly with my best friend and her husband who pastors our church. My tribe is large, the support is large for my father to bring him home to not miss any more birthdays, holidays and the love and care from his family and friends. Our church is directly involved with Prison fellowship, Angel Tree and re-entry. He will have the support of many. My father is not a threat to anyone, and is one of the most caring, God fearing men I have ever met. He loves the Lord and has never lost that seed that was planted in him as a young child and planted in me when I was young. He is almost 71 and I believe his release would give hope and restore a man who lost everything.

Thank you for taking the time to read this lengthy letter. I feel like there is so much more I want to say to share what a wonderful and God fearing father my dad is. I am confident that my support of my father would allow him to be a benefit to my family and my community. Time is ticking, and it has been a long road. I do not believe he deserves a life sentence. I thank you for your service and consideration in the release of my father.

In Him,
Amy Landers

• • •

To whom it may concern,

My name is Quovadis Marshall, I am the Lead Pastor of Hope City Church here in Waterloo. Hope City is a diverse congregation filled with people from many walks of life. Our church is located in Waterloo, Iowa. One of the things that makes Hope City unique is our partnership with local government, agencies and business. These strategic partnerships have allowed us to leverage our relationships and reap the benefits of the services and programs that our city provides for its citizens. This means, we have relationships with agencies that exist to help returning citizens integrate back into society, thus providing the vital and essential support system needed for success.

Based on my 20+ year relationship with Russ and personally witnessing the change of thinking, and perspective he has undergone leads me to believe that he is a great candidate for Compassionate Release. I believe that if released Russ would devote the remaining years of his life to strengthening the bond with his living children and forging greater bonds with his grandchildren. Our church has a number of peer and staff led support groups that we would ensure that Russ was participating in. We would seek to redeem the past bad decisions that Russ made by having him share his story in our juvenile diversion programs.

In light of these structures and opportunities, it is my belief that if released Russ would be able to integrate back into society and live the remaining years of his life as a productive citizen. Thank you for your consideration and for taking the time to read this letter.

Sincerely,
Quovadis Marshall
Lead Pastor — Hope City Church
118 High St.
Waterloo, Iowa 50703
myhopecity.net

1000 GIFTS FROM A 7 X 10

CHAPTER 15

Final Thoughts

On April 19, 2021, we were able to celebrate Dad's life in the very church he wanted to visit for so long.

I want to thank those who may have crossed paths with my dad over the years of his incarceration, those who were kind, those who showed compassion, and those who treated him like a human being.

I want to thank Kat and her team for fighting for my daddy until the end. Your compassion kept me looking forward and it was an honor to have someone like her in my corner.

I want to do better. I want us to "just do better." Compassion, empathy while maintaining dignity and public safety – can be done.

My daddy was not able to come home, this didn't have to be. He is still victorious, he still rests in the arms of my God, my Father in Heaven, and this I am sure of.

It was an honor, Dad.

24 years, 8 months, 1 day

296 months, 1 day

9,010 days

1,287 weeks

216,216 hours

2,927,960 minutes

178,377,600 seconds

The amount of time Daddy spent in Federal Prison as I walked with him through that journey.

There are more memories, incident, photos, and videos than what could be contained within these pages.

Follow me for more at:

Facebook: 1000 Gifts from a 7 X 10

Twitter: @1000gifts7X10

Tik Tok: @1000gifts7

Email: 1000giftsfroma7X10@gmail.com

Made in the USA
Middletown, DE
28 July 2025